A WORD DIFFERENT
THE BIG GREEN POETRY MACHINE

Poems From The South
Edited by Lisa Adlam

First published in Great Britain in 2009 by:

 Young**Writers**

Young Writers
Remus House
Coltsfoot Drive
Peterborough
PE2 9JX
Telephone: 01733 890066
Website: www.youngwriters.co.uk

All Rights Reserved
Book Design by Ali Smith & Tim Christian
© Copyright Contributors 2008
SB ISBN 978-1-84431-956-5

Foreword

Young Writers' A World of Difference is a showcase for our nation's most brilliant young poets to share their thoughts, hopes and fears for the planet they call home.

Young Writers was established in 1990 to nurture creativity in our children and young adults, to give them an interest in poetry and an outlet to express themselves. Seeing their work in print will encourage them to keep writing as they grow, and become our poets of tomorrow.

Selecting the poems has been challenging and immensely rewarding. The effort and imagination invested by these young writers makes their poems a pleasure to enjoy reading time and time again.

Contents

Applemore College, Southampton
Zoe Ferris (15) 1
Ryan Sherwood (13) 1
Craig Whettingsteel (15)
  & Emily Worsdale (14) 2
Andrew Thomas Mabbett (13) 3
Yasmin Di Carluccio (12) 4
Libby Biffin (12) 4
Eleanor Goodson (13) 5
Jamie Purkis (15) 5
James Luscombe (15) 5
Nick Whittle (15) 6
Stephanie Wells (15) 6
Lizzie Brown (15) 7
Jack Cole (13) 7
Lydia Ann Hansford (13) 8
Charles Burgess (11) 8
Lewis Teague (14) 8
Samantha Monaghan (12) 9
Phoebe Meredith (11) 9
Oliver Labram (13) 9
Timothy Blundell (11) 10
Rachel Hart (11) 10
Lisa-Marie Gray (15) 11
Jessica Biggerstaff (13) 11
Katharyn Pennell (12) 12
Alix Trenerry & Hannah Richards (11) . 12
Josh Trenerry (13) 12
Brittany Welham (11) 13
Zoe Waterman (11) 13
Alexander Andrassy (13) 14
Fleur Grace Hodgson (13) 14
Alice Clayton, Debbie Lentle
  & Katy White (13) 15
Nathan Dewey & Kerrie Hagon (13) 15
Dan Kitson & Jamie Brown (15) 16
Amy Rowan & Vicki (15) 16
Alex Wheeler & Curtis Pike (15) 17
Samuel Steven Keeys
  & Joshua Capstick (15) 17
Steph Parsons & Mark Brokas (15) 18
Natasha Crump (15) 18
Hanna Hunt & Jake McHugh (15) 19
Sophie Lloyd & Hannah Snook (14) 19
Mark Robins (15) 20
Matthew Routledge (11) 20

Blackheath High School, London
Alexandra Slater (12) 21

City of London School, London
Jack Clayton Clowes (11) 21
Yuri Colmerauer (13) 22
Rhodri Gillham (14) 23
Timothy Crawford (13) 23
John Casey (14) 24
Henry Thomas (13) 24
Ollie Bolderson (13) 25
Zizhou Zhang (13) 25
Max Packman-Walder (13) 26
Charlie Gladwell (13) 26
Thomas Visscher (13) 27
Kelvin Jayamaha (11) 28
Oscar Mahony (11) 28
Jonah Cowen (11) 29
Michalis Inglessis (12) 30
Oscar Humphreys (11) 30
Paul Fredericks (11) 31
Coronelli Marco (11) 32
Samuel Meah (11) 32
Mohsin Abedi (11) 33
Benny Myers (11) 33
Dougal Rea (11) 34
Richard Brice (11) 34
Alex Panagiotopoulos (13) 35
Boris Patrick Pagliaro (11) 36
Harrison James Jones (11) 36

Dover College, Dover
Lauren Clifton (11) 37

Eggar's School, Alton
Amy Lucas (12) 37

Harlington Upper School, Harlington
Laura Mackey (13) 38
Alexander Bandtock (13) 38
Charlie Pepper (13) 39

Highdown School & Sixth Form Centre, Reading

Gemma Cummings (11) 40
Lucy McCabe (11) 40
Megan Whittingham (11) 40
Ellis Evans (11) 41
Phoebe Bryant (11) 41
Helena Good (11) 42
Perran Moore (11) 42
Jake Streatfield (11) 43
Daniel Tanner (11) 43
Calum MacLeay (11) 44
Yemaya Lee-Hewitt (11) 45
Liam Tollafield-Davis (11) 45
Zahra Uddin (11) 46

Kingsdale Foundation School, London

Ellie Ross-Layne (12) 46
Meryem Osman (12) 47

La Sainte Union Catholic Secondary School, London

Nina Okocha (12) 47
Emma Benson &
  Ania Irena Busiakiewicz (13) 48
Valentina Okolo (15) 49
Emma Caggiano (13) 50
Ariadna Silva Chavez
  & Scarlet Vasconcellos (13) 50
Carianne Annan (13) 51
Brooke Davies (12) 52
Paula Field (12) 52
Ninotchka Rai (12) 53
Megan Shannon (12) 53
Molly Wiltshire (12) 54

Lingfield Notre Dame Senior School, Lingfield

Jacob Chenery (13) 54
Sam Ransom (13) 55
James Narula (13) 56
Gabriella Blake (13) 57
Max Elphick (14) 58
Charles Dawson (14) 59
Samantha Cruse (14) 60
Alex Hagel (15) 61
Tim van Riel (14) 61
Luke Wynn-Jones (14) 62
Joanna Hoggins (14) 63

Lewys Evans (15) 64
Jack Henderson (14) 65
Abbey Francis (14) 66
Kyriacos Cotonou (14) 67
Stephanie Harbour (14) 68
Imogen Bowen (12) 68
Maddie Thompson (14) 69
Will Barlow (13) 70
Kirsten Munday (13) 71
Chiara McDermott (14) 72
Hannah Hart (13) 73
Conor McIntosh (13) 74
Saskia Ingham-Jerrey (13) 75
Emily Malkin (13) 75
Josh Hampson (13) 76
Luca Alari-Williams (13) 77
George Hehir (13) 78
Amber Davey (13) 79
Hannah Gill (12) 80
Rachael Batory (12) 81
Josh Davison (12) 82
Megan Jones (12) 83
Tom Hawney (12) 84
Kate Pugh (12) 85
James Sterritt (12) 86
Thomas Gray (12) 86
Isabelle Ellis (12) 87
Jessica Dunn (15) 88
Matt Griffin (14) 89
Eden Medcalf (14) 90
Ben Wilson (14) 91
Beth Allard (15) 92
Emma Donegan (14) 93
Christopher Aris (14) 94
Laura Hookway (11) 94
Zeena Kerai (11) 95
Trisha Nayee (11) 96
Hamish Goff (12) 97
Mackenzie Simpson (11) 98
Isabel Hazelton (11) 99
Emily Cornish (12) 100
Maddy Groom (11) 100
Charlotte Hall (11) 101
Thomas Corbett (11) 102
Edward Willment (12) 103
Demi Barnes (11) 104

Alice Clutterbuck (12) ... 105
Madison Cahill-Smith (11) ... 106
Shannon Bridger (12) ... 107
Emily Bassett (11) ... 108
Jessica Dickins (12) ... 109

Notre Dame Senior School, Cobham

Beata Borelius-Larson (12) ... 110
Joanna Simpson (12) ... 110
Alex Adams (12) ... 111
Charlotte Robeson (12) ... 111
Alexandra Lee Harvey (13) ... 112
Gloria Nyangiye (12) ... 112
Lucy Walters (11) ... 113
Tilly Prowse (11) ... 113
Olivia Astles (11) ... 114
Isabelle Stewart (12) ... 114
Melina Klein (11) ... 115
Sarah Shutt (11) ... 115
Isabelle Cook (11) ... 116
Natasha Williams (11) ... 116
Allegra Gordon (11) ... 117
Imogen Alexandra Boffin (11) ... 117
Rachel Bertie (11) ... 118
Charley James (11) ... 118
Lorna Hughes (11) ... 119

Prior's Field School, Godalming

Sasha Kennington (11) ... 119
Emma Kendall (11) ... 120
Holly Morganti (11) ... 120
Harriet Thacker (11) ... 121
Sophie Jane Evans (11) ... 122
Charlotte Hardy (11) ... 122
Alexandra Paule (11) ... 123
Kelly McCall (12) ... 123
Rebecca West (12) ... 124
Maddie Demaine (11) ... 125
Lucy Stocks (11) ... 125
Eleanor Lunt (11) ... 126
Anna Sligo-Young (11) ... 127
Yolanda Foo (11) ... 128
Lydia Jarvis (11) ... 128
Nicole Harper (12) ... 129
Holly James (11) ... 130
Alex Lucy (11) ... 130
Abbey Prichard (11) ... 131
Samantha Sutton (11) ... 131
Miema Baker (12) ... 132

Sophie Field (12) ... 132
Molly D'Angelo (12) ... 133
Emily Milton (12) ... 133
Ellen Bryden (12) ... 134
Genevieve Labuschagne (12) ... 135
Jemima Sexton (12) ... 136
Evangeline Clery (12) ... 137
Ella Carey (12) ... 137
Susannah Whitmarsh (13) ... 138
Julia Parison (12) ... 139
Kimi Worsdell (12) ... 140
Harriet Martin (12) ... 140
Ella Briscoe
& Rebeccah Webber (12) ... 141
Katherine Oliver (12) ... 141
Charlotte Sullivan (13) ... 142
Sarah Quinton (12) ... 142
Millie McKee (11) ... 143
Charlotte Goodfellow (11) ... 143
Chesca Loggia (11) ... 144
Alice Budge (11) ... 144
Anna Hudson (11) ... 144
Farrell Cranstone (12) ... 145
Melissa Price (12) ... 145
Emma Droutis (12) ... 146
Amy Crawford (12) ... 146
Lois King (12) ... 147
Hanna Stephen (12) ... 147
Kate Alexander (12) ... 148
Amy Craig-Wood (12) ... 148
Ellen Ferguson (12) ... 149
Tamara Chiltern-Hunt (12) ... 149

Rowdeford Special School, Devizes

Stuart Boulton (15) ... 150
Matthew Goodyear (15) ... 150
Julian Emery (15) ... 151
Jake Sidwell (15) ... 151

St Peter's RC High School, Gloucester

Joshua Gasan (12) ... 152
William Thomas (12) ... 152
Nick Kowal (12) ... 153
Ellie Lister (12) ... 154
Sinéad Dangerfield (12) ... 154
Jem Winter (12) ... 155
Josh Mustoe-Linnane (12) ... 155
William Murphy (12) ... 156
Cameron Morgan (12) ... 156

Joseph Jennings (12) 157
Katy Coughlan (12) 157
Ollie Edwards (12) 158
Theo Neuschwander (12) 158
Lucy Keal (12) 159

Sandringham School, St Albans

Henry Cole (13) 159
James Riding (12) 160
Lydia Spooner (13) 160

Tewkesbury School, Tewkesbury

Kerry Dyer (12) 161
Kate Brookes (12) 161
Lesley McDowall (13) 162
Hannah Ballard (12) 162
Lauren Pickford (12) 163

The Arts Educational School, London

Holly Squires (12) 163
Marie Claire De Voil (11) 164
Colbert Newsome (13) 165
Ella Stephens (11) 165
Antonia Blakeman (13) 166
Georgia M Elvin (11) 166
Eve Burns (13) 167
Freddie Mark Anthony (13) 167
Emilia Campanale (13) 168
Mei Borg-Cardona (12) 168
Whitney Svosve (11) 169
Grace D'arcy Craig (13) 169
Yasemin Alkan (13) 170
Arthur Williams (13) 170
Susannah Pike (12) 171

The Buckingham School, Buckingham

Conor Tychowski (11) 171
Aidan Deeney (11) 172
Jasmine Swain (12) 172
Megan Horsler (11) 172
Paul Booth (11) 173
Katie Wood (11) 173
Daniel Rainsbury (11) 174
Holly Tucker (11) 174
Connor Luke Bennett (11) 175
Simon George (11) 175
Harry Akerman (11) 176
Georgie Gibbard-Bray (11) 176

Stephen Ettery (13) 177
Stuart Ironmonger (13) 177
Kayley Roberts (14) 178
Megan Thompson (13) 179
Marcus Prodanovic (13) 180
Rhiannon Taylor (13) 181
Emma Brazier (14) 182
Bryony Foote (13) 183
Robert Lukey (13) 184
Abigail Young (13) 185
Jade Heritage (13) 185
Amber Wieland (13) 186
Hayley Siklodi (14) 187
Lucy Piosek (13) 188
Gaia Ward (13) 189

The Hazeley School, Milton Keynes

Jack Balch (11) 190
Sophie Robertson (12) 190
Liam Coleman (11) 191
Lucy Abraham (11) 191
Amy Hewitson (11) 192
Charlotte Straker (11) 192
Georgia Barnes (11) 193
George Boland (12) 193
Dana Davey (11) 194
Gail Dechochai (11) 194
Emma Hoare (11) 195
Emily Brown (11) 195
Rebekah Harris (11) 195
Taylor Gordon (11) 196
Abigail Bernabe (11) 196
Adam Marshall (11) 197
Catherine March (11) 197
Tom Woodroofe (11) 198
Shai Barrett (11) 198
Courtney Doyle (12) 199
Jack Hurley (11) 199
Rosie Scott (12) 199
Lewis Hope (11) 200
Justine Connolly (11) 200
Oliver McCafferty (11) 201
Tom Flaherty (11) 201
Matthew Nelmes (11) 202
Megan Newman (12) 202
Shannon Leigh Wedley (12) 203
Sian Orange (12) 203

Lewis Orpwood (11) 204
Joe Lawson (11) 204
Rinnah Bassey (11) 205
James Knight (11) 205

Thomas Knyvett College, Ashford

Georgia Sue Matthews (11) 206
James Sutherland (11) 206
Jade Ayers (11) 207
Kista Gurung (11) 207
Arianne Dyett (11) 208
Hayley Sewell (11) 209
Raisha Hussain (11) 210

Tormead School, Guildford

Sarah-Jane Stedman (12)............... 210
Helena Coombs (12) 211
Sarah Barrett (12) 211
Madeline Roberts (12)..................... 212
Chloë Potter (12) 212
Katherine Badman (12) 213
Müge Ercis (12) 214
Katie Duxbury (12) 214
Stephanie Palmer (12) 215
Katherine Thomas (12) 216
Pip Scott (12)................................... 217
Victoria Marland (12) 218
Abigail Whall (12) 219
Alice C True (12).............................. 219
Caroline Davies (12) 220
Georgia Scott (12)............................ 221

Westergate Community School, Westergate

Estelle McLellan (13)....................... 222
Hannah Hill (13) 223
Zac Rigby (13) 223
Danni Noble (13).............................. 224
Lianne Cronk (13) 224
Keziah Norrell (13)........................... 225
Cameron Howell-McIntyre (13) 225
Faith Poston-Miles (13) 226
Jake Simpson (13)........................... 227
Nicola Ann Parfoot (13) 228
Gemma Williams (13)...................... 229
Ben Root (13) 230
Holly Anne MacWhirter (13) 230
Danny Vaughan (13)........................ 231
Jake Enticott (14) 231
Michael Long (13) 232
Kathryn Follis (13) 233
Gemma Thomas (13)....................... 234
Bill Bailey (13).................................. 235
Emma Morphy (13).......................... 236
Daniel Morgan (13).......................... 237

Wheatley Park School, Oxford

Ruby Nicholls (11) 237
Issy Standley (11) 238
Ana Majdi (11).................................. 238
Shakur Gabbidon-Williams (11) 239
Regan Cullen (11) 239
Davy Byrne (11)............................... 239
Jessie Green (11) 240
Victoria Montgomery (11) 240

The Poems

The World We Live In

The world we live in is bad these days
There are people taking drugs and drifting into a daze.

There is always fighting
With people kicking and biting.

Oh! isn't this the place to be
Look out the window and see black smoke from a chimney.

There is, on TV, always bad news
And 'good' people who have no clues.

So to the world we live in, we're sorry
And we'll work on it, so don't you worry!

Zoe Ferris (15)
Applemore College, Southampton

Environment

E ntirely independent, but not in use
N ature needs nurture, the key to the future
V iolently nature rules
I n our hands, we can save it
R evolving over time, we come, we go
O ver seas, great powerful seas
N ew to the world, try to help
M aintain the Earth to a natural way
E vergreen trees, falling down
N ever alone, we can all do something
T ogether we can help to save the world forever and ever!

Ryan Sherwood (13)
Applemore College, Southampton

Polluted Alphabet

A is for air, we need it to breathe
B is for bark, it comes off the trees
C is for cities, they light up the night
D is for danger, it's right in our sight
E is for environment, it's going away
F is for forest, it goes down each day
G is for greenhouse, the greenhouse effect
H is for hope, that we need to protect
I is for interest, we're losing it fast
J is for justice, a thing of the past
K is for killing, we do it for fun
L is for life, it's turning to run
M is for money, disaster it brings
N is for noises, from terrible things
O is for oceans, they're big, wide and blue
P is for pollution, that thick sticky goo
Q is for quiet, it rings through the night
R is for restless, the animals fight
S is for silence, it's not really there
T is for terror, the animals share
U is for uproar, the dodos are gone
V is for violence, we all know it's wrong
W is for war, the thing that we do
X is for xenophobia, which some of us show
Y is for yesterday, the things that have happened
Z is for zero, the time we have left.

Craig Whettingsteel (15) & Emily Worsdale (14)
Applemore College, Southampton

A World Of Difference - Poems From The South

Enough's Enough

Andy Mabbett's the president, he was voted in last year,
Once we children got the vote, we made our intentions clear;
Democrats; Republicans, they simply left us cold,
Andy was the one, because he's only twelve years old!

Us children, we won every senate seat, and Andy runs every state,
Now it's law for ice cream to be free on every plate;
Movies cost nothing, that's the way he wants things done,
He knows how to run the US for future and for fun!

Kids outnumber adults and tomorrow's ours you see,
Oldies made a mess of Earth, go look at history;
Killed the seas, polluted air and they really wrecked the land,
Now the planet's ours it's getting better, oil is banned!

Andy doesn't hold a grudge and never cares for profit hikes,
Games and toys prioritised with sports and pets and bikes;
Television thought it had us fooled with all its little lies,
Kids see the world through different eyes.

Andy shut down NASA, adults said he'd gone too far,
Then Andy used that money to perfect the solar car;
Oil tycoons complained of profit loss and falling shares,
Andy sent a memo: 'Go and tell someone who cares!'

Now that war has stopped, the army's cut to almost none,
Only a policeman is allowed to own a gun;
Street gangs are disbanded now, it's goodbye for the mob,
No one turns to crime 'cause everybody has a job!

Andy cancelled the nuclear program,
And the nation gave their thanks,
Then Andy shot all lawyers and he shut down all the banks;
They were making money for the ones who didn't need,
The one thing Andy never understood was adult greed.

Everybody's happy now, (except George Bush)
Air is clearer every day as children's power is pushed;
Kids deserve a future with an ocean, sky and stuff,
Listen to the growing voice of youth: enough's enough!

Andrew Thomas Mabbett (13)
Applemore College, Southampton

Our Earth

We have the sun, we have the snow
But because of us
That will one day go
We have the poor, we have the rich
We have the healthy and we have the sick
What we would do to have a cure
But because of us
Our world is ill and not pure
We hope someday that good will come
And rewrite the wrong we have written in our Earth's sum.

Yasmin Di Carluccio (12)
Applemore College, Southampton

Have You Ever Wondered?

Have you ever wondered,
Why the world is breaking down?
Why the world is in darkness
And the smell of pollution is lingering around?

Have you ever realised,
How we can really save it?
How we can definitely help
And that we can change this? We can change this now.

Have you ever done something,
Done something about the world's torture and pain,
Turned the taps off when not being used,
Or switched a light off in the day?

Things like this can really help
To improve the world,
Even something as small as picking up rubbish
Can make a huge difference, so help the Earth!

Libby Biffin (12)
Applemore College, Southampton

The World

Being environmental is good for us all,
If we look after the world,
Then it won't fall.
If we were to stop all litter,
Take it away, clean it up,
The world would be much fitter.
If we were to stop cutting all trees,
Leave them alone to live,
Then the world would be free.
So if we do give a damn,
Can we save the world?
Yes, we can.

Eleanor Goodson (13)
Applemore College, Southampton

Refutation - Haiku

Pollution and greed,
Denial and self-interest,
It's all our own fault.

Jamie Purkis (15)
Applemore College, Southampton

Innocence

Streaks of white,
in unbroken skies.
There they stay,
their imprints a lie.
For they seem to be harmless,
they're silent and still.
But their pollution you see,
destroys ozone at will.

James Luscombe (15)
Applemore College, Southampton

Colourful Scene

Green luscious grass,
Blue energetic ocean,
Orange uplifting sunset.
The world is a colourful scene.

Yellow touching sand,
Red succulent apples,
White innocent clouds.
The world is a colourful scene.

Black pouring oil,
Grey angry skies,
Brown devilish pollution.
The world is a darkening place.

Nick Whittle (15)
Applemore College, Southampton

A Black And White World

The ocean blue,
Overwhelmed and shadowed by pearlescent pools.
Aquatic creatures distant from the fairy tale
As tanks of oil barge through the sleeping seas.

The forest green,
Now burnt with the Devil's spear.
Animals' cries echo,
Whilst their young perish.

Brothers and sisters.
Enemies at war.
Why?

Gazing around
My sorrowed eyes weep;
The destruction created
Will decide our fate.

Stephanie Wells (15)
Applemore College, Southampton

Our World

The ocean is treated like a giant monster
Just waiting for its next rubbish meal
Little does it realise, it is really damaging itself.

The beautiful country is treated like a rubbish dump
Just waiting to be ruined
Little does it realise, soon there won't be enough room.

The glistening polar ice caps are treated like a melting pool
Just waiting to engulf our wildlife
Little do they realise, our world will no longer be.

Although with all the bad points in the world
The people are a team, just waiting to work together
To make the world a better scene.

Lizzie Brown (15)
Applemore College, Southampton

Greenhouse Gases

G ardens
R eaching
E nding
E verything dying
N othing
H ere just
O pen spaces
U ntouched
S urrounded by
E verything once upon a time.

G ames spoiled
A s is
S urrendering
E arth as it
S adly wilts away.

Jack Cole (13)
Applemore College, Southampton

The Earth's Song

T he world's going to end, if you don't think
H elp yourself by being
E conomically friendly

E arn your life, save the environment
A nd walk for freedom
R ighteousness will come
T he world's going to end
H elp yourself and others
S ave people's lives

S ave the world
O pen a new gate
N ow the way to freedom and life
G reenhouse gases are the main cause of our suffering!

Lydia Ann Hansford (13)
Applemore College, Southampton

Earth

E veryone can help
A ct now before it's too late
R espect our planet
T he world will one day disappear
H elp everyone by not helping yourself.

Charles Burgess (11)
Applemore College, Southampton

World - Haiku

People of the world
I do all my best for you
You give me nothing.

Lewis Teague (14)
Applemore College, Southampton

A World Of Difference - Poems From The South

What Are We Doing?

We are given the world to care for and protect
We take forward disuse and neglect
You don't see God walking into a brick wall
So why neglect the world at all?
We think about ourselves and I
When God just sits down to cry
Why oh why do we struggle to help?
And stop to think about someone else.

Samantha Monaghan (12)
Applemore College, Southampton

Our Earth

I give you power
You give me desire
I give you animals
You give me skeletons
I give you plants
You give me roots
I give you strength
You give me weakness.

Phoebe Meredith (11)
Applemore College, Southampton

The Way Of The World

The disastrous sludge, dripping out of contaminated pipes
Runs into the innocent oceans, killing fish . . . all types
And as the climate slowly heats up
We realise the world we are in is corrupt.
As we look into the eyes of Greed
We discover we are losing the resources we truly need.
To save the world, we don't need gratitude
All we really need is, to change our attitude.

Oliver Labram (13)
Applemore College, Southampton

Destroying Our Earth - Haikus

Our world is changing
The trees will soon disappear
The Earth will be gone.

Now quarries will rule
Planes, trains, cars will take over
The sky will be gone.

Problems are rising
Now peace will never return
The world is dying.

Timothy Blundell (11)
Applemore College, Southampton

Heartbroken

Animals lying on their side distraught
No one's around!
Children die, suffering, no good
No one's around!
Poor trees, no life
No one's around!
Ice blocks melting, no home for poor polar bears
No one's around!
Our planet is dying.

Rachel Hart (11)
Applemore College, Southampton

Gone

The world these days,
It's like people are in a daze,
They turn a blind eye
And the next minute we all die.

Pollution, pollution, pollution,
Litter and crime,
Maybe it will get better some time.

Now there's more danger,
We need more forest rangers,
Cows, horses, foals and animals,
Are dying all day long from no vegetables.

Lisa-Marie Gray (15)
Applemore College, Southampton

Without A Thought

The beauty of the world is taken for granted,
The respect for the world hasn't even started,
We go on day by day pretending to love
But the world has just about had enough.

The flowers we look at every day
Are simply beautiful in every way
Nature is around us everywhere
But we don't take time to stop and stare.

But my point of the poem is very clear
We just sit back and enjoy a beer
We just watch the world being destroyed in front of us
Without a care, without a glance, without a thought.

Jessica Biggerstaff (13)
Applemore College, Southampton

Tick-Tock

Tick-tock
Second by second
Minute by minute
Hour by hour
Day by day
Bang!
There goes the world
Mankind's chemicals
Have killed us!

Katharyn Pennell (12)
Applemore College, Southampton

Earth To Earth

Darkness swarms all over the world,
A creepy sound echoes through all the towns,
Nothing but the battle of pollution.

Pollution, pollution, pollution,
What is it doing to our world?
Pollution, pollution, pollution,
The Earth is going wild.
Pollution, pollution, pollution,
It is affecting us all.

Alix Trenerry & Hannah Richards (11)
Applemore College, Southampton

A Dream

Over the hills and far away,
Lives a little girl who wants to say,
Stop polluting and save the day,
Otherwise the world won't be gay,
So please save the world today.

Josh Trenerry (13)
Applemore College, Southampton

Pollution

Lakes full of garbage,
Animals disappearing.
Air turning green.
Pollution, pollution.

People coughing,
Toxic waste.
Rubbish all over the place.
Pollution, pollution.

Losing family,
Living in the dark.
Smelling fumes from gas.
Pollution, pollution.

Brittany Welham (11)
Applemore College, Southampton

Pollution

P lanet dying,
O xygen decreasing,
L akes, rivers,
L ives lost,
U ntidy sea,
T rees burning,
I ce melting,
O verheating,
N on-stop!

Zoe Waterman (11)
Applemore College, Southampton

What Happened?

I used to own a strong hill,
I have it no longer,
It's now used as a landfill.
My rainforests used to be stronger,
They were the victim of a kill.
My rivers used to flow,
They flow no more,
They stopped a long time ago.
My birds used to soar,
Forests should not glow,
Birds soar no more,
The seeds of life, we must re-sow.
My humans used to be kind,
For a new home . . .
They will not find.

Alexander Andrassy (13)
Applemore College, Southampton

Turning Pollution

I look around and see this world in perfect harmony
But when I think about it harder
I really start to see
The damage that we're doing
The pain our world can feel
I wonder what simple things
We can do to slow this wheel
I hope and pray
That just one day
People might begin to see
The damage that we're doing
Please help save us, set us free.

Fleur Grace Hodgson (13)
Applemore College, Southampton

Pollution

P lease, please
O ur planet needs help
L ook outside and in your home
L ots of things to be done
U se your energy efficiently
T ogether we can save the world
I n the future we can make it work
O ur planet needs your help
N othing can stop us now!

Alice Clayton, Debbie Lentle & Katy White (13)
Applemore College, Southampton

Pollution Solution

P roblems
O verpowering
L itter
L eaving
U s
T error-stricken
I n
O ur
N vironment

S aving
O thers'
L ives
U sing
T eamwork
I ntelligently.
O utcome:
N o turning back!

Nathan Dewey & Kerrie Hagon (13)
Applemore College, Southampton

Once Upon A Time

Once upon a time there was a beautiful land
(There is a horrible, smoggy land)
Full of lush green grass and a bright blue sky
(There is a muddy field and a gloomy sky)
Animals running freely
(There's not a panda in this place)
The man goes past, pulled by a horse
(A coach goes by, propelled by black fog)
Birds migrate from country to country
(Bombs inflict death between nations)
This is how it was, this is how it could be
This is how it is. We've all heard of change!

Dan Kitson & Jamie Brown (15)
Applemore College, Southampton

Those Poor Polar Bears

This is how the story begins.
A mother polar bear and her twins,
Trampling through that soft white snow.
They turn around what d'ya know?
Their world has melted, everything gone,
This is when they realise they've not got long.
The ice caps have disappeared,
Their home's destroyed,
If I was a polar bear, I'd be annoyed.

Amy Rowan & Vicki (15)
Applemore College, Southampton

The Earth Is Mourning

The Earth is warming
That's its warning
It's full of pollution
Without a solution
The Earth is mourning
As the end is dawning
Our doom will be seen
Unless the world turns green
We depend on the trees
Or we will all freeze
So don't cut them down
Or we will drown
As the ice caps are melting
'Cause the temperature is sweltering
So let's change our ways
Or say goodbye to our days.

Alex Wheeler & Curtis Pike (15)
Applemore College, Southampton

I Am The World

I am the world
I am dying
You are killing me
With your CFCs
I am the world
I am dying
You are destroying my moons
With your toxic fumes
I am the world
I am dying
You are making me choke
With your thick black smoke
I am the world
I am dying.

Samuel Steven Keeys & Joshua Capstick (15)
Applemore College, Southampton

Breath Of Life

The trees are meant to be green,
but from what I have seen,
we are polluting
and we are recruiting
the bad of this world.
What can we do
to make this world true?
For here we shall live,
will you help us give
this world a new breath of life?

Steph Parsons & Mark Brokas (15)
Applemore College, Southampton

A World Without Light

The sun in the sky,
Where has it gone?
All I see is smoke,
Where is it from?

The whole world is dark,
Full of smog.
I am now underground,
Buried next to my dog!

Natasha Crump (15)
Applemore College, Southampton

Stealing

You take my beautiful trees
You turn them into shreds.
I tell you, stop this please.

You take my gorgeous seas
You turn them into pools of pollution.
I tell you, stop this please.

I'm on my knees.
Stop! Begging you please.

I am the Earth
Don't hurt me.

Hanna Hunt & Jake McHugh (15)
Applemore College, Southampton

Environment

E ngland needs to stop pollution
N eeding to stop litter
V ile smells everywhere
I need to do something
R ubbish everywhere you go
O vercome the disaster to this world
N otice how much pollution is around
M otivate in helping out
E nding up with a better world
N ice that you have helped us
T he environment needs you!

Sophie Lloyd & Hannah Snook (14)
Applemore College, Southampton

Clean Environment

C lean up the world
L et it live
E ven if you have to work harder
A nd help us be a greener country
N ever let it happen again

E verybody does it
N o one can stop it
V ictory is not in our sight
I n our point
R ubbish should be binned
O ur future wants a clean country
N ow we are cleaner
M ost of us want to stay that way
E veryone helps
N ow that people won't forget
T hat we are a green country.

Mark Robins (15)
Applemore College, Southampton

Pollution

In the world up in the sky there is a deep black hole.
Inside there is a beast with the breath of Hell.
Slowly rotting our world and licking his lips for flesh and much more.
If only people looked around and could see the damage they have done.
There could be no beast wrecking our world and there could be life.
So many things that just are too pretty to describe
And we could be happy.

Matthew Routledge (11)
Applemore College, Southampton

Recycling

R educe, reuse, recycle every day,
E co-friendly is the way,
C ans, glass, paper, let's end this strife,
Y ou can help for a greener life,
C ars, planes and boats, let's ban them all,
L iving with pollution will be the Earth's fall,
I f we all recycle today,
N othing can harm the planet this way,
G oing green will help the Earth, so remember to recycle!

Alexandra Slater (12)
Blackheath High School, London

Mourning In Wootton Bassett

Here they come,
Like black ants slowly marching around puddles,
Inching through traffic,
A cortege cut up by impatient motorists,
Oblivious to the sacrifice of these silent soldiers,
Some only 20, and still 50 miles from their final resting place,
This is no highway for heroes.

No flags, no police escorts flank their route.
Only the weary town residents recognise their bravery,
Standing in line again to pay their respects,
While the gleaming cars glide solemnly past.
Shopkeepers and office workers step out and bow their heads.
At the war memorial a cluster salutes,
Blazers faded, berets lowered, buttons polished,
A homecoming nobody wanted.

Jack Clayton Clowes (11)
City of London School, London

The World

The world was . . .

an equal place
a balanced place
no pollution
no extinctions
nothing that will jeopardise
its existence
until homosapiens
came along
the smartest of all
species
changed the world
for his benefit.

The world is now . . .

crowded with humans
ice caps melting
a lot of pollution
poor countries with no education
an unbalanced place
with its existence at stake
people help to think of ways to
reduce their carbon emissions
and help others to save their
homes and families
who will be manly
enough to save us?

Who?
Is it you?

Yuri Colmerauer (13)
City of London School, London

Hope

I hope I can add a little pique,
To my upcoming critique,
I hope I will have a beautiful world to preserve and live in,
Not one of the office blocks, that is like a bin.
For one thing I wish, that at least you would be so kind,
As to leave us some fish to find.
Please cut out the incessant fighting,
Because the world, it is biting,
And at last, I hope,
That you will leave us some hope, and not too,
About the destruction of our world, to mope.

Rhodri Gillham (14)
City of London School, London

Gas Guzzler

I just have to confess, I made a big mess
I bought a gas guzzler . . . and now for the puzzler

It's shiny and smooth and boy can it move
It's got air con 'n' sat nav, drink holders to spike
But there's one big fat problem that no one could like

It's all very well drivin' round like a swell
But we can't just let the world go to hell!

We've gotta learn to save what's left of our oil
Else future generations will do nothing but toil

Only one solution occurred to me,
I'll just have to sell it and use ol' Shank's pony!

Timothy Crawford (13)
City of London School, London

Green For Our Planet

Green is a colour,
Green is a style,
Green for our planet,
It may take a while!

Green like a lizard,
But not like a snake,
Green for our planet,
How long will it take?

Green like the algae
On top of a pool,
Green for our planet,
We learn it at school.

Green can be solar,
Electric or wind,
Green for our planet,
Or not at all.

John Casey (14)
City of London School, London

The World Going By

I switch on the TV, waiting for fun
But all I get is the news.
I watch it anyway,
Watching the disasters around the world,
War, tsunamis, gangs and killings,
All around the world,
Everyone is watching
But not one does a thing.

Henry Thomas (13)
City of London School, London

Wars, Poverty, Racism

Wars
Never-ending wars,
People die and people hurt,
Over trivia.

Poverty
Poverty is real,
People who can't afford food,
Always left hungry.

Racism
Racism hurts,
Anger over colour?
Could you get any lower?
Idiotic,
Stupid,
Malicious.

Ollie Bolderson (13)
City of London School, London

Eco Limerick

We only have one world in this life,
So please, try and keep it nice.
Don't drop litter on the floor,
You'll like it all the more,
When the future looks lovely and bright.

Zizhou Zhang (13)
City of London School, London

Over The Top

The dark before dawn
The dread before morn
No time to pray
The first shot of an endless day
Where killing is currency

Over the top, over the top
My legs are getting tired
Over the top, over the top
The only way out
Is to *run* away from the battle
Your comrades in peace beside you
The chaos soon ignites
But we carry on the fight

Over the top, over the top
Will this nightmare ever stop?
Over and over and under my skin
Their sights are the only thing we cannot be in.

Max Packman-Walder (13)
City of London School, London

I Roll Along

I roll along that long clean line
All of us together
We get split apart and onto shelves
And put into your leather.

You click me open, drink my fluid
And then thrown upon the ground
You walk on me
You crumple me
But later I am found.

I am with plastic bags, bits of can
And even roadkill
Later we are all dumped
On that dreaded landfill.

Charlie Gladwell (13)
City of London School, London

A World Of Difference - Poems From The South

The World Is My Oyster

The man picked up his knife and fork
He ordered the animals for starters
He scooped whales out of the sea
And snatched rhinos from the land
And scraped up tigers from the jungle
With his nails he wiped them clean
And there were none left
'But I'm not full yet!'
He said

He wiped his mouth with the sleeve
Then the main course was natural resources
He gorged his coal with speed
And ate up the oil without pause
And rushed down his rainforest-greenery salad
Blood-sap seeping from his chops
And there were none left
'But I'm not full yet!'
He said

Now the big man was thirsty
There's plenty to drink here
So he gouged down the oceans
And sloshed round the seas
And swallowed all the lakes and rivers
In one huge gulp
And there were none left
'But I'm not full yet!'
He said

He licked his lips at devouring desert
That brown wasteland that lay barren before him
So he munched at the flecky, crumbly Earth
And licked the muddy insides out
And scoffed the last few crumbs of his meal
While burping and farting all the time
And there was nothing left
'But there's nothing left to eat now!'
He said.

Thomas Visscher (13)
City of London School, London

Environmental

E verlasting trees - they are threatened by the everlasting effect of pollution.
N ecessary action is required to protect the environment.
V isual beauty is destroyed because mankind has cut down the rainforests.
I ce and igloos are starting to melt because of the increase of global warming.
R ecycling - we need to recycle our paper to help the environment.
O paque - dark opaque colours are taking over the sky because of mankind.
N ecessary action is required.
M ankind block out the natural scenery.
E ndless - endless pollution from cars. Mankind doesn't care about this.
N othing - nothing can compare to the fact that mankind is destroying the world that God gave us to look after.
T rees need our help, mankind is destroying them.
A nd amazingly the world hasn't been destroyed by people not caring about the environment.
L itter makes our streets unpleasant to walk in.

Kelvin Jayamaha (11)
City of London School, London

The End Of My Life

I was running, running for my life,
How could the operation have gone that wrong?
I turned around, got a German in my sight and fired,
He fell as quickly as he had appeared.
Suddenly a burning pain in my right leg,
I went down screaming,
I could see the glint in the German's eye,
As he fired, the bullet hammered into my heart,
And then, peace.

Oscar Mahony (11)
City of London School, London

The Nuclear Bomb

It destroys cities
It ruins landscapes
What is it?
The nuclear bomb

Nothing withstands it
Nothing survives it
What is it?
The nuclear bomb

It causes death
It causes grief
What is it?
The nuclear bomb

Hiroshima
Nagasaki
What is it?
The nuclear bomb

Life: none
Happiness: none
What is it?
The nuclear bomb

No fear, no worry, life, joy
What is the difference?
A bomb-free world.

Jonah Cowen (11)
City of London School, London

Spite

They point and laugh, they make fun of me.
It feels like I've been stung by a bee.
But it pains me more than any bite,
For what they say is pure evil and spite.

What makes me different with brown eyes?
Will anyone now hear my cries?
What makes me different with black skin?
We all do wrong and we all sin.

They say Martin Luther King sorted it all out,
But they don't know what they're talking about.
If you look at me - a black-skinned boy
Who's treated like a dog's play toy.

Let's make a world where we're all the same
No matter our skin colour, eyes or name
Let's make a world where I can be free
From pain and teasing and misery!

Michalis Inglessis (12)
City of London School, London

Rats

Running, running, running
Over plastic bags and under packaging
The smell of bad eggs is rising
There must be a better place than this.

Running, running, running
Through puddles of who knows what
The sound of seagulls cawing
There can't be a worse place than this.

Running, running, running
Over broken furniture and through a rusty fridge
All around me is rubbish
There should be a better place than this.

Running, running, running
Through used clothes and shoes
They feel all wet and stiff
We have to make a better place than this.

Oscar Humphreys (11)
City of London School, London

A World Of Difference - Poems From The South

The Litterbug

Monday morning:

I got on the tube today, onward to Liverpool Street.
I had all the carriage to myself and I thought, *what a treat!*

Across the land I travelled, more and more people got on,
But someone dropped their can of Coke.
I said to myself, *that's wrong.*

Tuesday morning:

Again I got on the train today, about to walk out the door,
When all of a sudden, a packet of crisps,
Covered up half of the floor.

Wednesday afternoon:

I was coming home from school today, I needed to make haste,
I looked out over the river and gasped,
For it was full of toxic waste.

I saw a glimpse of a figure, like the dark side of the moon.
The litterbug had struck again, I swore I'd get him soon.

Saturday lunchtime:

I went to London with my dad,
Who was talking about a whetted knife.
I yawned and looked at a field, the junk was killing plantlife.

The land was becoming a filthy place,
And most people feared the worst.
There was so much rubbish that stretched from London,
And lead right up to Buckhurst.

Sunday evening:

It seemed the litterbug had won the week, but luckily for us,
The government had many recycle bins and gave them all to us,

All through the night we worked, and the very next day,
London was clean and the litterbug caught.
Hip hip hooray!

The moral of this tale is just to say,
Recycle or throw your rubbish away.
For it be a sin, if you didn't put it in the bin.

Paul Fredericks (11)
City of London School, London

Homeless/A Muslim Woman - Haikus

Homeless
Forlorn on the street,
Why need wait for tomorrow
If none cares for me?

A Muslim woman
I can see you all,
Can you see through my burka?
Can you see my heart?

Coronelli Marco (11)
City of London School, London

How To Be A Super Eco-Hero

Mirror, mirror I call
On the wall.
How can I
Become the greatest superhero of all?

Well, you can't get powers in under ten hours.
But you still can be super like me,
Become the greatest superhero that can be.

Why don't you reduce the waste?
Like from the trash bin and toothpaste
That is a way to
Become the greatest superhero that can be.

Why don't you reuse?
Like pieces of paper and the old lamp fuse.
That is a way to
Become the greatest superhero that can be.

From Gran's motorcycle
Why don't you recycle?
Reduce, reuse and recycle are the actions
Of the greatest superhero anyone can be.

Samuel Meah (11)
City of London School, London

A World Of Difference - Poems From The South

What Will Our World Be Like Tomorrow?

What will our world be like tomorrow?
I often lie at night and wonder . . .
Will there be green fields and farms for animals
Or will it all be a black smoke because of pollution?
Will there ever be peace on Earth between countries,
Religions, cultures or will there continue to be horrific wars,
Innocent casualties . . .
Acts of random terrorism?

What will our cities be like tomorrow?
As I walk to school, I look around and often wonder . . .
Will the hustle and bustle be a happy joyous one
Or will people be scared to go out
Because of the rising knife and gun crime?
Will I see smiles on faces around me
Washed in colours of the rainbow
Or will the dark greyness of racism and murder dominate the city?

What will the children of today be like tomorrow?
When I see myself growing up in this carnage, I do wonder . . .
If the future can be bright for the children playing in the parks
Or will poverty and homelessness prevail?
Will we ever step in and make an effort to stop this injustice
Or will we continue to go about our way,
Doing our school work, securing our future?

What will our world be like tomorrow?
I worry, I get angry, I continue to wonder,
But for now, I live today in the best possible way
And hope for a better tomorrow.

Mohsin Abedi (11)
City of London School, London

Recycling - Haiku

Garbage has piled up,
Earth resources need our help.
We must recycle!

Benny Myers (11)
City of London School, London

Litter Is Bitter

I thought I saw a silver ring that sparkled in the sun.
I looked again and saw it was the wrapper from some gum.
I thought I saw a treasure map, that promised jewels and gold.
I looked again and saw it was some newsprint, torn and old.
I know there is a world out there, free of dirt and litter.
If only we lived in that world, I would not feel so bitter.

Dougal Rea (11)
City of London School, London

The Unfortunate Man

This is my terrible land, my depressing town
And here is where I wear the poverty crown

I sit on the street corner, my head in my hands
Hoping to hear my cup chink as money lands

My pride and joy is my sleeping board
I didn't pay for it, that's the best I can afford

As I walk along people point at me
They whisper, they talk, then they flee

I walk into the chicken joint; it's time to eat
I sit at the bar and tear into the meat

It's time for bed and I stroll back to my den
Knowing the next day will be like the last ten

I am the unluckiest homeless man of all
In this great big world, I feel very, very small.

Richard Brice (11)
City of London School, London

Global Warming

I once read a good magazine
Which was terribly, terribly keen
On ensuring that we,
When boiling some tea
Did it in a way that was green.

It said we should fill up a mug
With water procurred from a jug
Which we then pour in
To a kettle which then
Is used to heat the water up.

The reason to do it the way
It urged us to I shall now say,
It seemed every drop
That we boil takes a lot
Of energy from far away.

I put the paper down on a chair
And then I sat up to stare
At the humming fridge
And the sloshing dishwasher
The lights, which were on
The meal, which was cooking
The telephone, which was ringing
The computer, which was charging
And the red TV light
And the electric piano
And the plastic cutlery
And toys
And boxes
And trays
And everything in the house
And then I gave way to despair.

Alex Panagiotopoulos (13)
City of London School, London

Hiroshima - Haiku

A busy Monday
Blinding light, hot as the sun
Eighty thousand die.

Boris Patrick Pagliaro (11)
City of London School, London

The Canvas

In a lone skyscraper stands a canvas painting,
The only surviving human artefact on this Earth.
Surrounded by a cesspool of ruins and abandoned cities,
Around which is the water caused by climate change.
The canvas shows what life should have been like,
For the people and animals on this planet.

Seas of parkland and nature reserve, interrupted by islands.
Small islands of property development.
Wind farms stand tall surrounded by water and beach.
A beach on which everyone can play.
Animals roam around the beautiful country pastures,
With no plough attached to their back.
Children playing happily in the streets and parks, with no cares in the world.
With no fear of teenage street gangs.

The picture on the canvas never became a reality,
Inside this tall skyscraper of Earth.
In a world destroyed by Man in many ways,
This canvas shows what could have been.
If Man had left his greed behind,
And saved the environment he lived in.

Harrison James Jones (11)
City of London School, London

The Dreadful Dream

You see a table and a chair,
A crystal ball a gleam.
See Earth in time in outer space,
The lighting all a beam.

No footsteps of the polar bear,
Their homes gone, without a trace.
No snow or ice, it's just all gone,
Because of the human race.

If we all pull together,
We can all create
A better future
And a greater fate.

Lauren Clifton (11)
Dover College, Dover

The Planet

I am a place of mysteries,
I am a place of shining waters,
I am a place of ancient ruins,
I am a place of soldiers' quarters.
I feel a love, of many meanings,
I feel the warmth of many seas,
I feel an anger, of many thoughts,
I feel a dream of many memories.
I have a life of guiding people,
I have a life of exploring the wild,
I have a life of hills and valleys,
I have a life of women and child.
I am a world of life and death,
I am a world of whisper and voice,
I am a world of peace and joy,
Let me live or die, that's your choice.

Amy Lucas (12)
Eggar's School, Alton

Why Is There Racism?

We could work together in unity
Or respect each other's beliefs
But some people don't in the world.
   Why is there racism?

From different places around the world
But all really the same person
We are not that fair to them.
   Why is there racism?

Remember Martin Luther King
He began the no-racism reign
Some of his thoughts have floated away.
   Why is there racism?

Just different coloured skin
That's all you need for bullies
They just don't leave others alone.
   Why is there racism?

One day we all do hope
That there will be unity
Working together, with each other
   There will be no racism!

Laura Mackey (13)
Harlington Upper School, Harlington

The Polar Ice Caps

Silence, a single drop
Water flows
From the ice
Water flows
Into the sea
Water flows
From my wrist
Water flows
I am melting
Water flows
I am gone.

Alexander Bandtock (13)
Harlington Upper School, Harlington

The Bully In My School

There's a bully in my school,
He always pokes me in the hall,
He calls me fatty four-eyes,
Cos there's a bully in my school.

When I'm on my way to classes,
He always makes fun of my glasses,
I don't know what to do,
I end up hiding in the loo,
Cos there's a bully in my school.

He seems to haunt me in my sleep,
He makes me always want to weep,
It's driving me to Hell,
I don't know who to tell,
Cos there's a bully in my school.

Nobody seems to really care,
All they tend to do is stare,
The fear is killing me,
But nobody can see,
Cos there's a bully in my school.

I've tried so hard to hide the fears,
But now I'm choking on the tears,
I try my best to hide,
The secret locked inside,
Cos there's a bully in my school.

I feel like walking out the door,
I can't take it anymore,
Will it ever end?
The damage will never mend,
You'll never know the pain involved,
Or how this issue will resolve,
I'm feeling like the fool,
Cos there's a bully in my school.

Charlie Pepper (13)
Harlington Upper School, Harlington

Don't Be Mean, Go Super Green

Go green, don't make a scene
Don't be mean and go super green!
The world is dying and nothing's being done
Go green, it's much more clean!
Everyone could help together
To make the world so much better
Go green, go super green!

Gemma Cummings (11)
Highdown School & Sixth Form Centre, Reading

Don't Be Mean, Go Green

Go green, it's a bit more clean
Especially if you don't litter.

Go green by using bags from your last shop,
You should feel much, much better.

Go green by home recycling
It's easier than you think.

Go green, not pink.
It's not that embarrassing.

So go green,
It's really not that hard!

Lucy McCabe (11)
Highdown School & Sixth Form Centre, Reading

Go Green, Don't Be Mean

Streetlights flicker,
Engines roar,
Litter flitters and floats across the pavement,
People die,
Birds can't fly,
All because of the fumes,
How did we get to this?

Megan Whittingham (11)
Highdown School & Sixth Form Centre, Reading

The Earth Needs A Friend

The Earth needs a friend
It begs, 'Please don't send me to my end.'
My sea is being polluted every day
Please don't let me die this way.
My little animals big and small are now being hunted down
Please don't kill my little pets, every time one dies I frown.
My big green fields are being overrun
Please don't overrun my fields, I feel like I'm being hung.
My body is not feeling swell
Please just stop and make me well.

Ellis Evans (11)
Highdown School & Sixth Form Centre, Reading

Go Green

Everyone go green,
Please don't be mean,
Make the world a better place,
Don't be afraid to show your face,
To make the world a better place.

Recycle everything you can,
Try to make some use out of a metal can,
Reuse all your plastic bags,
We don't want any tags on our country,
So make the world a better place.

Phoebe Bryant (11)
Highdown School & Sixth Form Centre, Reading

Ways To Help The Environment

There are lots and lots and lots of ways
To help the environment recover
Here's a list of the smallest things
That will change the world for the better
The first one is to recycle your cans
And all your other junk
Number two is to turn off your taps
You'll save a lot of water
Number three is to turn out the lights
As you leave the room
Number four is to walk and walk
Instead of using the car
So there's a list of little things
That can make a big difference
Here's one more I almost forgot
The most important one of all is . . .
Save trees, ban homework!

Helena Good (11)
Highdown School & Sixth Form Centre, Reading

The World Is Dying

We need to be eco-friendly
As pollution is deadly
You hear the children crying
As the world is dying.

Don't chuck litter
The water's bitter
You hear the children crying
As the world is dying.

The governments lie
While polar bears die
You hear the children crying
As the world is dying.

Perran Moore (11)
Highdown School & Sixth Form Centre, Reading

Go Green

A long time ago the Earth was green
The most beautiful place
Ever to be seen.

It once was a paradise
So naturally clean
And can be again
If we go green!

So dump your car
Don't buy too many things
Put all your rubbish into rubbish bins.

Jake Streatfield (11)
Highdown School & Sixth Form Centre, Reading

Every Little Helps

Recycle, reuse, regenerate
The world could be a better place
If we could just reuse paper
So we leave more trees standing
And we can also recycle things
Such as paper, bottles, boxes
And many more things
So we can help save the planet.

Daniel Tanner (11)
Highdown School & Sixth Form Centre, Reading

Change The World

Change the world.
Let me see the floor
Without all this litter.
Get rid of air that tastes bitter.
Let me see the air without smoke.
Let the factories go green or kill me.

Many of us try
But there is not much hope for others.
Every little thing helps the world
So change and go green.

Change the world.
Get rid of plastic bags.
Make bags yourself to save the world.
Stop using cars and use a bus to help the world.

Many of us try
But there is not much hope for others.
Every little thing helps the world
So change and go green.

Change the world.
Trees and trees fall for no use.
Sure it makes nice furniture
But how would you like to suffocate?

Many of us try
But there is not much hope for others.
Every little thing helps the world
So change and go green
And let the world see hope.

Calum MacLeay (11)
Highdown School & Sixth Form Centre, Reading

A World Of Difference - Poems From The South

Don't Be A Mess, Keep It Fresh!

There are so many ways,
That you can be green,
And so many ways
That you can be mean!

But what you should do
Is just think,
Of all that rubbish that sinks.
Maybe this stuff is a bit too much spending,
But no one will mind doing a little lending!

Yemaya Lee-Hewitt (11)
Highdown School & Sixth Form Centre, Reading

I Don't Understand

I don't understand,
Why the government makes planes costly,
Why don't we do something different?
Why don't we just make fewer but bigger planes,
So we can fit in more people?

I don't understand,
Why we advertise things that waste energy,
Why don't we do something different?
Why don't we stop advertising wasteful things
And advertise games and sports?

I don't understand,
Why we watch TV,
Why don't we do something different?
Why don't we read books
And socialise?

I *do* understand,
Why we should
Stop and think,
So we can all
Save the world.

Liam Tollafield-Davis (11)
Highdown School & Sixth Form Centre, Reading

Go Green

Don't leave lights on,
to keep our environment clean.
Reduce your carbon emissions,
help the world by going green.
Stop cutting down trees and don't litter,
do these things to make life on this planet bigger.
Don't waste paper or plastic bags,
reuse them again if you can.
Don't keep the electricity running or water either,
cycle to school and make this world
a better place for you and me.

Zahra Uddin (11)
Highdown School & Sixth Form Centre, Reading

Homelessness Poem

H ungry and tired.
O verhead I hear people laughing and joking, I wish I could join in.
M y energy levels get lower and lower by the minute.
E veryone ignoring me, pretending they can't see me,
   almost as if I'm invisible.
L onely and desperate, desperate to be loved.
E veryone walking past. 'Change?' I say. 'No,' they say.
S cared some maniac or young lads could come and attack me.
'S orry,' they say when I ask for change.
N obody knows my story, nobody cares.
E nergy levels seriously low, decreasing by the minute.
S omebody stop and help, someone take pity upon me.
S cared and alone, just a normal day I guess.

P eople muttering curses under their breath as they walk on by.
O vertired and freezing right down to the bone.
E xcited when someone gives me change,
   it's like I've won a million.
M oney is all I want, money, money, money.

Ellie Ross-Layne (12)
Kingsdale Foundation School, London

Homeless Poem

Lonely and cold, no one to go to,
Nowhere to stay.
Just homeless.

I'm out here in the cold,
Begging for some money.
Give a coin, give me something,
Something to last me throughout the night.

I'm fighting for my life,
Fighting for my rights.
I guess I'm on my own,
No nothing, just me and my sleeping bag!

Meryem Osman (12)
Kingsdale Foundation School, London

Why Me?

Why me?
Why can't I have fresh clean water,
A place to call home sweet home?
But instead I live in darkness,
I have nobody and nothing,
I call out for help but no one hears me,
I cry out for love but no one cries with me.
Why me?
I feel as if the world's crushing into pieces
With me in the centre,
I hope for happiness but sadness I get.
Why me?

Nina Okocha (12)
La Sainte Union Catholic Secondary School, London

The Wild

Animals fly, they fly so high
Jumping and gliding, running and hiding
Insects crawl so deep into the ground
Like silent mice making no sound
Sharks are known to be bad
Whales just always seem to be sad
Crocodiles laugh
While elephants bath
Monkeys swing
And all the birds sing
Nature is beautiful and great
Sometimes we even find them on our plate
While we're having fun
Animals' lives are done
Animals get hunted
Bad hunters need to be confronted
Some hunters don't follow the law
What are they doing this for?
Although it's the world that the humans rule
Why don't you just stop being so cruel?
Animals fly, they fly so high
Jumping and gliding, running and hiding
Insects crawl so deep into the ground
Like silent mice making no sound.

Emma Benson & Ania Irena Busiakiewicz (13)
La Sainte Union Catholic Secondary School, London

A World Of Difference - Poems From The South

The Conversation With The World

I went to speak to the world today
It seemed she had a lot to say
About us humans, our foolish acts
And from that she gave a list of facts
'I was created as your habitat
No legs or arms, just a diameter that's fat
To leave enough space for you all
So that the wonderful rainforests could grow tall
Yet you chop them down without a care
You burn them and so pollute the air
Then for your clothes and personal pleasure
You capture animals as if they were treasure
You bomb other countries, relentlessly
Leaving people homeless, causing poverty
You don't respect each other or show equality
There's racism, sexism and so much more I see'.
But *why?*
Are you pleased when your country goes to war?
If your rights were taken, would you say 'OK, sure'?
Aren't you bothered by our worldly destruction?
When a natural disaster occurs, do you pay attention?
And so on behalf of the world, I've come to say,
Appreciate this world every day.
Though you may not hear her speak literally
Be aware of effects you cause, mentally and physically.

Valentina Okolo (15)
La Sainte Union Catholic Secondary School, London

Earth

I'm proud to live on Earth,
I do what I can,
I pick up litter and recycle,
I even wash my clothes at 30.
Whoever is out there
Please listen and listen well,
The Earth is growing weaker,
And has not much time,
Take care of the Earth,
In so many ways!

Emma Caggiano (13)
La Sainte Union Catholic Secondary School, London

Oh, What Will We Do?

Ice caps are melting,
Drowning the Earth,
But no one is helping.
Oh, what will we do?

Gas and smoke polluting the Earth,
Suffering for those future births.
You won't appreciate things until they are lost,
Is that what the world will have to wait for,
Until they find out the extremely big cost?
Oh, what will we do?

The whole world isn't a scientist.
If there wasn't such ignorance,
The world is creating a death list,
We are the humans with brains,
We are the ones that are meant to change.

The world is everywhere we look,
But people seem to be so blind.
Through all the chances we took
Now we haven't got any chances to find.
Where will we look to?

Ariadna Silva Chavez & Scarlet Vasconcellos (13)
La Sainte Union Catholic Secondary School, London

Would You Really Care?

If the world was exploding tomorrow
Would you really care?
For other people's sorrow
Would you really care?
I bet you would but you're too scared to do anything
Oh yeah
Bet you'd be crying in bed trying to sing
Praying to Jesus and the King
Hoping they'd forgive your sins
Someone in this world is sheltering in the bins
But you're just at home not doing anything
They need your help
But would you really care?
If the world was exploding tomorrow
Would you really care?
For other people's sorrow
Would you really care?
Bet you would but you're scared to stop wasting nuclear power
Oh yeah
Saving energy by having a 3-minute shower
Then feel like you're on top of the world with all the power
If not, thinking about your last hour
With your family, that's so sour
Who aren't saving energy or power
Yes I'm saying would you really care
If the world was exploding tomorrow?
Would you really care
For other people's sorrow?
Would you really care?

Didn't think so
Because you're too slow
Or our environment should be
Something to show!

Carianne Annan (13)
La Sainte Union Catholic Secondary School, London

A Few Pence!

Another day on my own,
Begging, pleading for a home.
I sit here every day, all alone,
As people walk by.

They really don't care,
And they just stare,
So I tend to think
My life is unfair.

I usually get a filthy look or two,
As I dance and sing,
But I have to say to myself,
Hey, who cares
As I really need some money to pay the rent.

So I'll so anything just for a pound or two,
So help me discover there is more in this world,
As I am a young girl.
Please help, I beg of you!

Brooke Davies (12)
La Sainte Union Catholic Secondary School, London

Ice Melting

My name is Lola, I'm a polar bear
I don't come to hesitate or scare
I'm trying to tell you it's not fair
We haven't got a fish to spare.
So help today and you will see
All the polar bears be free!

Paula Field (12)
La Sainte Union Catholic Secondary School, London

No One Wants Me

No one wants me
I watch people sleep on their comfy bed at home
I cry for someone to hug me
I want someone to love me.
No one wants me
I want someone to protect me in the dark
I want friends
But I have no friends.
No one wants me
I want a best friend
I want to go to school to learn.
No one wants me
I'm just an orphan girl!

Ninotchka Rai (12)
La Sainte Union Catholic Secondary School, London

Litter Is Everywhere

Litter, litter, it is everywhere
Here and there and even at a fair
If it is not in a bin
Then it is a sin
Litter, litter, it is everywhere.

If you see litter, pick it up
Or put it in a cup
Put your litter in a bin
It will only take one min
If you see litter, pick it up.

Megan Shannon (12)
La Sainte Union Catholic Secondary School, London

Poverty

P ollution and litter, it will seem so bitter
O ften people don't know . . .
V ast amounts of animals will soon be extinct
E very man should stop and think
R acism and war, you all think it's a bore
T ry your best and help the rest
Y our time is limited, so make it worthwhile,
   so stretch that extra mile.

Molly Wiltshire (12)
La Sainte Union Catholic Secondary School, London

My World

I watched the news today
Each story worse than the last,
And I kept thinking to myself,
What is happening to my world?

War in Afghanistan,
Two British soldiers killed,
Afghanistan children left crying without parents,
What is happening to my world?

Famine in Ethiopia,
Limited water and food for all,
Yet the rich get richer,
What is happening to my world?

Another youth stabbed in London,
Another mother has to bury her son,
This just isn't right,
What is happening to my world?

We only have one planet,
You only get one life,
If we carry on like this,
The planet will not survive.

Jacob Chenery (13)
Lingfield Notre Dame Senior School, Lingfield

Chernobyl

1986 Saturday 26th April at 1.23

The city slept, but the fearsome reactor was awake
It was waiting for the moment
Then it struck with cruelty and maliciousness
1,000 tonnes of metal ripped itself off the ground.
It hurled itself through a concrete wall
Vicious chemicals, radioactive substances poisoned the air.
Bits of graphite, chunks of uranium fuel
Pieces of control rods were strewn around the floor
Two men died in the blast but that was just a starter
The fire had a raging appetite that needed to be satisfied
The fire was immense and seemingly unstoppable
For days the fire blazed and continued to fill the air with
choking chemicals
Over the following months some 30 others were to die
Most to perish were heroic firemen who gave their lives
The radiation burns and radiation sickness killed them all.
The death was caused from the unstable materials being used
After days the fire and radiation had started to recede
When the fire went out some order did return
The horror is etched in our minds forever.

Sam Ransom (13)
Lingfield Notre Dame Senior School, Lingfield

The Earth Is Dying

When people say the Earth is dying,
We don't believe them, say they're lying.
Landfill sites and rubbish dumps,
Piled up in heaps, humps and lumps.
Smell the rotting, see the waste,
Of this horrible, ghastly place.
The energy that goes to waste,
The batteries we change too soon, in haste.
What about the tasty food we leave,
Especially on Christmas Eve?

When people say the Earth is dying,
We don't believe them, say they're lying.
Wasted heating in a house, losing all the rays,
Closing doors and insulation, these are just two ways.
Hear the wind turbines whirling out at sea,
Generating eco-electricity.
Flick the switch and turn it off,
Save the power you have got.
When you think about what the Earth could become,
All you can say is that people are not lying,
And the Earth is really dying.

James Narula (13)
Lingfield Notre Dame Senior School, Lingfield

Aqua Contamination

Why do we do it?
Fill up the rivers
With sewage and waste
Water means purity
Not anymore
Why do we do it? Why?

Streams start from a tiny source
A little trickle of hope
Thin, clear drips of movement
Running down the mountainside
Why do we do it? Why?

Streams are small but rivers mighty
Swiftly dragging everything with it
Flowing fast to some great expanse
Of aqua - but we soon poison it
Why do we do it? Why?

Canals -
What would we do without them?
Great transport, great fun
Yet now they're merely oil slicks
Why do we do it? Why?

We can help
Stop littering the shoreline
Of the Channel and the Thames
Ugly factory mouths mustn't belch out these toxins
We can fix what we do, *now.*

Gabriella Blake (13)
Lingfield Notre Dame Senior School, Lingfield

What Have We Done?

The sun rises over the bleak wasteland like a god
Its radiance shining down and lighting up the Earth with hope
A lone figure walks across the blasted Earth
The Masai elder looks over the land.
He sits on the rough, hard ground of what used to be a paradise
And he weeps.

He sees death and destruction
He sees trees torn asunder by the greed of countless nations
He sees animals purged by selfish people who think nothing of life
It is the greatest betrayal that we who have been raised
and nurtured by Mother Nature
Turn on her in her hour of greatest need.

He sees the world exploited
Its resources sucked dry by greedy countries just as a child
might drink from a straw
The Earth is cut and gashed as humans hack at its crust
trying to find resources that should be left alone.
The land is polluted from innumerable chimneys
which belch their contents out over an innocent Earth
changing and warping whatever's in its path.

He sees suffering and hardship
He sees nations tearing themselves apart in wars
of their own making
He sees the strong prey on the weak like jackals.
He sees tyrants and dictators taking what is not theirs.
He sees mankind ripping apart the Earth and everything on it.
But most of all he sees people weeping
He hears their cries for help.

Most of all he hears Mother Nature weep
Her tears unheard by the masses
The roar of the chainsaw, the crack of the gun is all we humans hear

We destroy, we pillage, we burn
But we never give.
Only take what is not ours.

The Masai elder puts his head in his hands and cries.
What have we done?

Max Elphick (14)
Lingfield Notre Dame Senior School, Lingfield

It Wasn't Me

Films on TV, pictures in the press
Nag at our conscience and force us to think.
But if we don't listen to the truth
We can lie to ourselves to forget.

It wasn't me
Was it you?

Deaf to the cries of the starving child,
Blind to the suffering of the poor and weak.
Send in help with tanks and guns
And watch nations learn to hate.

It wasn't me
Was it you?

Destruction, disease, destroy our dreams
Holes in the ozone, holes in our hearts.
Pollution, confusion, disillusion, it's all the same.
We were too selfish to stop it or care.

It wasn't me
Was it you?

In 100 years from now I'll be ash and dust
Too late to correct what harm we've done.
We tortured the Earth as it screamed in pain
And surrendering in agony, we left it to die.

It wasn't me
It wasn't you
It was all of us
Are you proud?

Charles Dawson (14)
Lingfield Notre Dame Senior School, Lingfield

Do You Even Care?

Nothing's worth losing
Especially the chance
To make it right
So why do we insist on
Putting up a fight?
Peace and love
For this world you live in
So why do you only care if
You're the one who wins?
Life is hard
But not for you
People starving in
Africa, Uganda and
Orphans in Bulgaria
They're the ones who
Need you
To love, to care
To help
They can't live like that
But what can they do?
They're helpless
Starving
And they have no food
Do you even care
About these people in need?
Do
You
Even
Care?

Samantha Cruse (14)
Lingfield Notre Dame Senior School, Lingfield

Rainforests In Retreat

What is a rainforest?
What do you see?
From the smallest weed
To the tallest tree
The children of the future will not be able to see
The rainforests
If we keep cutting down the trees
We need to let people know that
If we keep cutting down the trees
The rainforests will not be there to show.

Alex Hagel (15)
Lingfield Notre Dame Senior School, Lingfield

What Are We Doing?

You've given us everything we need,
We're ruining it, with our greed.

All the animals, including the snail,
We're killing them all, without fail.

We're burning trees, they're all going,
We're stopping the rivers from flowing and flowing.

We're polluting the air and killing the bees,
We're melting the ice caps and raising the seas.

We need to stop or the world will die,
We're polluting the air and ruining the sky.

Tim van Riel (14)
Lingfield Notre Dame Senior School, Lingfield

Is There Any Hope?

Sea levels rising
People are crying
Everyone knows it
But no one wants to show it

World's getting hotter
And there's Harry Potter
Wasting our paper and ink
But no one wants to know it

Rainforests falling
Mountains are calling
There is no hope for us
If the trees, they don't stop falling

We could all stop this
If everyone helped
But
It would take all of us
Or we send the Earth to its grave
It will be the new world
And the old world would not be missed.

Luke Wynn-Jones (14)
Lingfield Notre Dame Senior School, Lingfield

Environmental Poem

Forests destroyed, lakes polluted,
Time goes by, the world flashes before us,
People need to open their eyes,
See what they're doing.

The population is growing bigger and bigger,
But yet we never think to differ,
We carry on and use up what we like,
But we never stop and think about the costs of life.

The waste we produce every year,
Is too much, we have to stop and think,
If we just recycled,
The world would be a better place,
With more room to plant trees
And time to watch bees.

Just think about the consequences,
That your family might have,
Just stop and look around at what is left,
It may not be around in 100 years' time,
So be the better person and don't do the crime.

Joanna Hoggins (14)
Lingfield Notre Dame Senior School, Lingfield

Denial

Why do we ignore the truth?
Does anyone seem to care?
We're killing the planet,
It's all our fault
And who do we choose to blame?
The fact is it's all going wrong.
We're in the middle of a crisis.
Why do we do it?
Is it because we have no respect?
Do we need to sit up and realise?
Is it because we're ignorant?
Is it just hunger for money and greed for power?
Do we have any consideration?
No, because we have nothing else to do!

Lewys Evans (15)
Lingfield Notre Dame Senior School, Lingfield

A World Of Difference - Poems From The South

We Just Can't Lose!

Look at the world we're killing,
Look at the world we're filling
With things which we have yet to use,
Everyone's waiting for their muse.

Their inspiration, their solution,
To help us all to stop pollution.

If leaders can't uphold the law,
How can they hope to stop before
It gets out of our hands to cease
And life itself we fail to seize.

Animals die and trees can burn,
But it is not this for which we yearn.
A cleaner world and a cleaner sky,
Could help humanity survive.

Natural disasters could be Earth's way,
Of telling us we're near Doomsday,
Where everything we've ever done,
We'll see destroy us, everyone.

Cars and trains and ships and planes,
All just keep adding to the Earth's pains.
An easy way to stop it all,
Is to stop burning fossil fuel.

Recycling plastic and paper and glass,
Could help us to refine life's class.
Some people say, 'It can't be true!'
But we still have to follow through.

The climate's changed and so should we,
This world's not the best it could be.
We can all stop it if we so choose,
If we *all* try, we just can't lose!

Jack Henderson (14)
Lingfield Notre Dame Senior School, Lingfield

Opposites

We have money
They have none
We have grass and flowers
They have sand and mud

We have water
They have none
We have food
They have rice

We have life
But they have death
They have poverty
We have none

We see happiness
They see sadness
We see light
But they see dark

We have heat
They have cold
We have love
They have each other

We have cosy beds
They have the hard floor
We have duvets
They have torn sheets

We have houses
With lots of rooms
They have one big room
For far more people

It's not fair!
They need help
They can't cope
On their own

We need to act now
Right now.

Abbey Francis (14)
Lingfield Notre Dame Senior School, Lingfield

Abrafo And White Man

Abrafo stood perched on a rock by his tree
                                        Staring white man in the eye.
Waving his arms above,
He shouted through his desert's emptiness
Like a man swept by fury.

Whilst snapping the branch that hung from the tree,
                                        White man took another
From the trees that stood tall
Amongst the once pleasant land.

Abrafo took his knife
From beneath his worn, white cloak,

To shave a sharp point at the tip of his branch.
Without haste,
Without thought,
Without care.

With one hand through his short black hair,

He made his way across the land
And swiftly pounced at white man,
                                        But the bullet was faster.

His rich blood poured from within the bullet holes,
Glimmering across his native skin.

But Abrafo is smiling,
As he is rid of his duty.

Kyriacos Cotonou (14)
Lingfield Notre Dame Senior School, Lingfield

My World

Corrosion, destruction, distress,
Lives lost and dreams crushed,
Sadness and anger upon people,
Poverty in our world.

This is reality. This is the world we live in.

War strikes, with children dying,
Blood as red as the pain inside broken hearts.
Tears to fill a pool of water,
Just how can you carry on?

This is reality. This is the world we live in.

Wasting necessities, water and all.
But have you ever stopped to notice the people in our world?
Flesh and bone. Rich and poor. Life and death.
Our world is falling apart.

This is reality. This is our world.

Stephanie Harbour (14)
Lingfield Notre Dame Senior School, Lingfield

War Is Wrong!

W ar is never-ending
A story never finished
R ifles at the ready

I watch people fall
S creams all around me

W ithin the battle
R ich and poor die
O nly I see the pain
N o one else cares
G rateful to be alive!

Imogen Bowen (12)
Lingfield Notre Dame Senior School, Lingfield

My Land

The sun shines,
The wind blows,
Spring is welcomed,
By the first rose.

The sky is blue,
The grass is green,
Summer appears -
A beautiful dream.

The trees are bare,
The earth is damp,
Autumn smells,
Of a fire camp.

The ground now hard,
The snow is white,
Short days of winter,
With little light.

How perfect can
My homeland be -
When just across the open sea,
Lie countries that could never be

As blessed as ours
For all to see, but instead -

Are full of bloodshed,
No sun, no water,
No food or bed,

Just 'war' left for those not dead.

How can this world
Not provide -
Equal life
For all mankind?

Maddie Thompson (14)
Lingfield Notre Dame Senior School, Lingfield

Contrast

Did you ever stop to notice,
The flourishing fields in summer,
Or the winter landscape, white as far as the eye can see?
Did you ever realise and think,
How could we possibly sacrifice this?

Did you ever stop to notice,
The blazing battlefields of Baghdad,
Or a desolate landscape, destroyed by what we've done?
Did you ever realise and think,
What was here before?

Did you ever stop to notice,
The crystal clear Hawaiian sea,
Or the mind-blowing Niagara Falls, a scene from Heaven?
Did you ever realise and think,
Are we wasting all of this?

Did you ever stop to notice,
The polluted urban seas,
Or the smoking factories in cities, a disgusting scene from Hell?
Did you ever realise and think,
I wish we had never done this.

Will Barlow (13)
Lingfield Notre Dame Senior School, Lingfield

Child Of Time

I am the child of the past.
Running outside and drinking in the fresh air,
Touching the trees
And feeding the birds and deer,
Smelling the flowers
And hearing the horse and cart wander by.
I am the child of the past.

I am the child of the present.
Walking outside and breathing in the air,
Touching the few surviving trees
And feeding the birds and deer in the enclosure,
Smelling the flowers, their scent dulled by fumes
And hearing the traffic trundling by.
I am the child of the present.

I am the child of the future.
Crawling outside, struggling to breathe,
Touching the houses where the trees had been,
Feeding the ghosts of the birds and deer,
Trying to breathe, but smothered by gas,
Hearing the cars, buses and trains rush by.
I am the child of the future.

Kirsten Munday (13)
Lingfield Notre Dame Senior School, Lingfield

Why?

Why do the fields run red with the blood,
Of battle cries, tossed in the mud?

Why do the seas choke on your waste,
Spitting waves try to rid the taste?

Why do you smother the skies with grey,
And grasp that self-worth that wanders astray?

Why do you turn the night into day,
Play with God's toys and say it's okay?

Why do you find so much peace of mind,
In burning the planet and all of mankind?

Why have the birds forgotten their song?
Why can't you tell what's right and what's wrong?

Why do you toy with genocide?
Who gave you the right to decide?

Why do you wait for time to melt away?
Why do you always do as they say?

Why do you dive into seas of mainstream,
Forget what it's like to think and to dream?

Why is tomorrow never today?
Why can't you face the price you must pay?

Why does nature turn away in disgust?

    I think you know why . . .

Chiara McDermott (14)
Lingfield Notre Dame Senior School, Lingfield

Everything Is Turning Black, Everything Is Dying

The green world is turning black,
The blue sky is turning black,
The yellow sun is turning black.
Everything, everywhere is turning black.

The trees in the forest are dying,
The elephants in Africa are dying,
The seals in the Antarctic are dying,
The people in the Third World are dying.
Everything, everywhere is dying.

Why?

Well, it's not the sun
And it's not the rain,
But it's no one else's pain to gain.
It didn't happen 60,000 years ago,
It only happened when we were born.
And again you ask why.
Look in the mirror,
Witness not the victim,
But the murderer.

Hannah Hart (13)
Lingfield Notre Dame Senior School, Lingfield

Earth

When I was born I was pure.
I was as pure as the snow that caps my mountains
And the rain that falls from my clouds.
Then came you.
You who are greater than the others,
You who could think for yourselves.
I thought you would care for me,
As I cherished and nourished you.
My diamond sky was soon filled,
With your cloaking, burning gas,
As black as night.
You who cut down my giants,
You who carved out my hills.
Your machines of metal tear up my land,
Only to kill the one you seek.
The forests you have burnt to feed your anger.
My children who roam the Earth,
Were killed by your fire.
I feel my energy ebbing.
If I must go, then so must you.
If I must die, then so will you.

Conor McIntosh (13)
Lingfield Notre Dame Senior School, Lingfield

Our World Of War

War now dominates the streets of the world,
The possessions of children litter roads,
A ball, never again to be hurled,
The dead owner who used to use it loads.
Bodies of children and adults alike,
Cover red fields that used to hold blue flowers,
Soldiers in their tanks who don't want to fight,
But are controlled by a higher power.
The flashing lights of bombers in the sky,
Strikes fear in the heart of everyone,
The bombs come whistling down from on high,
Each one causing so much devastation.
Why continue to do this to our Earth?
Think of the children who used to have mirth.

Saskia Ingham-Jerrey (13)
Lingfield Notre Dame Senior School, Lingfield

Earth Poem

What a shocking sight,
Trees falling,
Animals dying,
Pollution ruining the atmosphere,
All for what?

For unnecessary pleasures,
For paper that is wasted,
For ivory and skin and meat that is not essential,
For light and heat which we can get from the sun and the fire.

It is preventable and we can all help
Get our environment back to the way it was,
Green trees, wild animals roaming free,
Blue skies and clear horizons.
That's what God intended.

Emily Malkin (13)
Lingfield Notre Dame Senior School, Lingfield

The World

That cool breeze on a hot summer's day
That whistles through the trees,
The perfectly shaped white snowflake
That drifts to the ground with ease
The sweet song of the first spring bird
Returning to its nest
And the midsummer sunset
Re-igniting the west

The vast oceans so pure and blue
That swallow up the sun
And the tall and mighty mountains that block it out for fun
The baked savannahs of Africa
That stretch into the haze
And the lush and vivacious rainforests
Where it pours for days and days

All of these magnificent things
Will soon be black and dead
The whole of the world
Is sleeping on a toxic bed
It's not too late to save the world
But time is running out
Recycle, turn off your lights
And help Mother Nature out.

Josh Hampson (13)
Lingfield Notre Dame Senior School, Lingfield

The War Poem

It was time, we were going over,
I marched onwards, keeping with my squad,
The ground was just thick mud,
Every step we took was with caution,
Trying not to sink into the brown mud,
The dark smell of gunpowder hung in the air,
Penetrating my nostrils.
Suddenly, gunfire erupted through the air,
I saw the squad in front of me being thrown to the mud.
Is there really a winner in war?
Bullets ripped through the air,
Shredding innocent men to pieces.
Is there really a winner in war?
Before I knew it, I was on the floor,
Blood spilling out of me as I sank into the deep mud.
Is there really a winner in war?
As I sank, I thought about all the millions of soldiers,
The soldiers that have given their lives
And the soldiers that will give their lives in future wars.
Is there really a winner in war?
I closed my eyes and that was the end.
Is there really a winner in war?

Luca Alari-Williams (13)
Lingfield Notre Dame Senior School, Lingfield

Mother Earth Is Dying

Mother Earth is our life
Mother Earth is our home
Mother Earth is ours
Why are we ruining her every passing day?
Without her we are nothing
We are killing her every day
Every tree that is cut down
is a mark left on her once natural skin
Every animal that is poached is a hair pulled out
Every war that destroys mankind is a bruise left on her body
Every single piece of waste that is thrown out onto her streets
is slowly decreasing the age that she will live to
Every emission is a gas that is stopping her breathe
Every single resource that is being overlooked
is dampening her vision
Mother Earth is barely surviving
Her face is becoming ugly
Her body is turning weaker
We have to help her
Otherwise she will die along with us.

George Hehir (13)
Lingfield Notre Dame Senior School, Lingfield

I Wish

I wish we were back in the day,
When animal walked alongside Man,
When we treated them as equals,
When there were more of them than us.

When things were basic but good,
When there was enough food and water,
When we only ate when we had to, and
When we did - the food was clean.

When the weather controlled itself,
When we weren't changing it,
When the conditions everywhere were bearable,
When everyone had the same.

When there was green everywhere,
When the air smelt fresh,
When we ran barefoot and
When there were more trees than people.

Before the wars,
Before the pollution,
Before the racism,
Before we destroyed the world.

Amber Davey (13)
Lingfield Notre Dame Senior School, Lingfield

Safari Sadness

The girl looked out of the jeep's window
As they bumped across the African plains
The zebras spooked and galloped away
As the lions roared their arrival.

The black rhinos snorted warily
And threw their grand heads to the sky
The sun glinting on their horns
As they trotted sedately by.

The guide was describing clearly
How all these animals were thriving
But then if only they knew
What the bleak future would bring.

As the rest of family talk busily
As they fly back home towards England
The girl thinks to herself
What a wonderful world . . .

The pretty young woman
Gazes out shockingly
As the rusty jeep speeds past
The rhinos are gone and the lions are thin
The grass is brown and dry

Her children ask her
Where the animals are
She answers 'I don't know'
But deep inside
She screams out loudly
With despair for what humans have done.

So why do people do it? she thinks
Why do they kill the animals?
As they go back home on the plane
She says 'This is terrible'.

The old woman and her grown-up kids
Look sadly on towards
The dying animals, the suffering plants
The desert and desolate land.

Where the animals were are bones
Where the grasses were their ash
Everyone crying and sad
The creatures reduced to shadows.

So think before you act
And if you listen to that
You'll perhaps not see what the lady saw
And not regret yourself seeing.

Hannah Gill (12)
Lingfield Notre Dame Senior School, Lingfield

Hope

Rivers of toxin flow out to the sea,
All life is snared; no one is free,
This desolate land is full of despair,
And no one can help; nobody's there.

Spirits of loved ones look on in dismay,
Knowing the truth that we'll have to pay
For the damage we've caused, hunger and greed,
We need someone to follow, someone to lead.

There is hunger and war, sadness and dying,
People alone, bereaved and crying.
Earth's spirit joins us in a howl at the moon,
We lost all hope, all dreams, too soon.

But maybe we can all make a change,
Although some faults are out of our range.
At least we can try, try to repair,
The damage that we left, and make some things fair.

Though summer whispers are just memories,
It keeps us going, through winter's breeze,
We're running out of time, no time to mope,
What strengthens our hearts is hope.

Hope.

Rachael Batory (12)
Lingfield Notre Dame Senior School, Lingfield

The Credit Crunch!

The world is being destroyed,
People are becoming unemployed,
People are not having lunch,
Because of this credit crunch.

Countries becoming poor,
It's something you can't ignore,
The government is collapsing,
But some people are just relaxing.

The UK is getting smaller,
By 1% says the caller,
If only the government can decide,
How much money to provide.

This is really getting bad,
No more money, which is sad,
This world is turning into a scrunch,
Because of this credit crunch.

Josh Davison (12)
Lingfield Notre Dame Senior School, Lingfield

War

Dying brothers
Sobbing mothers
Funeral costs
People are lost

Guns and battle
Machine-gun rattle
Revolver shots
People time forgot

Children slaughter
Forgetting laughter
The sky is black
People never coming back

Fields of war
Never wanting more
Wars never won
People are gone

Houses destroyed
No playing boys
No crazy dares
People worse for wear

Disappearing stories
Now nothing but gory
Nowhere to play
People are fading away

Our future is awful
Always dreadful
What if we could just stop?
Now that would be top, wouldn't it?

Megan Jones (12)
Lingfield Notre Dame Senior School, Lingfield

Eco Poem

We take the world for granted
Destroying plants we planted
We hardly spare a thought
For animals captured or caught

Killing, murder, suicide
All the laws we don't abide
War is tearing the world apart
Evil people, evil hearts

The world is almost ruined
By humanity's awful doings
Gases fill the air
Not many people care

The news is always talking about
Many animals dying out
Orang-utans and panda bears
With the animals we must share

So let's start to take care of our planet
We are very lucky we still have it
Let's save the world - let's do it with haste
To make the Earth a better place.

Tom Hawney (12)
Lingfield Notre Dame Senior School, Lingfield

Environmental Poem

The world, what a wonderful place,
The sun glows brightly across the Earth's face.
The flowers sway silently in the morning air,
The animals sleep peacefully, without a care.

The world, what a dull land,
Flowers are gone, silent and sad.
The trees are falling down to the floor,
The small forests can take no more.

The world, what an unhappy place,
The animals are gone, it's an empty space.
No birds fly through the air,
The animals have gone, it's not fair.

The world, what a noisy land,
War screams and shouts across grass and sand.
People get hurt, blood is shed,
Everyone is sad, people are dead.

The world, can we improve this land?
Can we make good what is bad?
If we recycle and make things great,
It's up to you, decide the world's fate.

Kate Pugh (12)
Lingfield Notre Dame Senior School, Lingfield

Global Warming

Global warming, it's such a sin,
To think we've made the ice so thin.
The seas will rise before our eyes,
Acid rain falls from the skies.

The Poles will melt,
The heat is felt.
The planet's getting hot,
Believe it or not!

No more snow at Christmas time,
The snowy days are far behind.
All summer spent in the shade,
Because of all the heat we've made.

Because we have been so careless,
Who in the world will protect us?
Because of the emissions we've made,
Some people are becoming afraid.

Of all the things we could have been,
Couldn't we have started green?

James Sterritt (12)
Lingfield Notre Dame Senior School, Lingfield

Polar, Polar Bear

White and really furry
Leaves in a hurry when
Polar bears are good swimmers
They're one of the winners
But their habitat is being ruined
By us leaking oil into it from our ships
They like to eat a big meal
That is their best deal
They're hairy, big and strong
But they're not scary, even though they're ten feet long.

Thomas Gray (12)
Lingfield Notre Dame Senior School, Lingfield

Alone

Floating eternally in outer space
We mustn't divide, we are but a single race
We are alone with no one to help but our own helping hand
Upon this Earth of mud, sea, sand

The animals are suffering
We are creating their pain
As well as chopping down forests
Causing acid rain

The rivers are trashed
And little is cash
For the world is a cruel place to be
We are polluting
And seeking and shooting
For the world is a cruel place to be

Global warming is making us sweat
But whose fault, who is to blame?
All we can do now
Is to make changes, but how?
As a little goes a long way

Recycling and more
Shoos the trouble from our door
So give a thought today

We are alone, but life isn't fair
But that is no reason to ignore and not care.

Isabelle Ellis (12)
Lingfield Notre Dame Senior School, Lingfield

The Cursed Fate

Playing in the H_2O
Splash of my flipper, *splish* of my fin
Bubbles erupt about me
In their shimmering masquerade
Chasing the silvering fish
Up and down
Round about
Over and over again
What's this? It must be my lucky day
Fish as far as the eye can see
Hanging limply, tantalising, beckoning
Swimming, swimming, the rush of water in my gills
Yet I'm caught, checked, wire tightening about my skin
Struggle, the urge to breathe is great
Coming closer, closer, crushing darkness
The cursed fate.

Jessica Dunn (15)
Lingfield Notre Dame Senior School, Lingfield

Who Will Pick Up The Pieces?

Empty stomachs
Empty fields,
When all the children are crying
The backs are being turned.
> Someone will pick up the pieces.

The gaping hole in the ozone
Growing larger every day,
Something has to be done
Before it is too late.
> Someone will pick up the pieces.

The constant fighting around the world
Causing destruction and pain,
But losing all your loved ones
Is only part of the hurt.
> Someone will pick up the pieces.

Wasting the planet's resources
As if they'll all come back,
Time is of the essence
Wasting the world away.
> Who will pick up the pieces?

Matt Griffin (14)
Lingfield Notre Dame Senior School, Lingfield

The Machine

6am
I climb aboard the machine and the key turns,
Machine awakens and yawns
Monkey scales a tree as the machine begins its meal
A tree collapses and is devoured
The machine rages on
Monkey screams
The machine is hungry still
Miles of rainforest is eaten
The machine relentlessly continues
Fires rage and the forest is burning
The machine remains uncaring
7pm
And the key is removed
The human machine returns to its slumber.

Eden Medcalf (14)
Lingfield Notre Dame Senior School, Lingfield

Our World

There are extreme amounts of evil in our world,
There is so much pointless behaviour,
There are many people suffering in poverty,
There are also people with wallets that are always full of money.
It is disgusting how much upset inconsiderate people can cause,
They ruin homes and forests,
Many beautiful creatures of the planet live here,
Many tribes of thousands of years have their livelihood disrupted!
The people who seem to have everything are never happy,
Yet the people with nothing are all but sad faces,
That shows how mixed up the planet on which we live is.
The original way of the planet is broken,
There is no trust here anymore,
The world is full of pain and anger, panic and hardship.
Death means nothing to many people
And life is only a way of getting money!
The killing and murder that goes on is pointless,
People think it makes them big, but in fact it makes them small.
This is becoming a ruined place,
This is our world.

Ben Wilson (14)
Lingfield Notre Dame Senior School, Lingfield

Without The Earth

The Earth is the start of everything
Where life begins and ends
Be it animal, plant or mineral
And now it's up to us to make amends

Poverty, famine and global warming
Serious issues we shouldn't ignore
Ice caps melting and millions dying
Endangered species and much, much more

We need to preserve our Earth
And now is the time to pay
So future generations can enjoy the world
Which is slowly diminishing each day

Without the Earth, we wouldn't exist
Without the Earth, there'd be no you and me
Without the Earth, we'd have nothing
Without the Earth, where would we be?

Beth Allard (15)
Lingfield Notre Dame Senior School, Lingfield

Our Generation

We take it for granted
We live for today
Never tomorrow, or the day after
Or next century.
Next century
Our children could be asking why
Their parents left nothing
No tree left standing
No fuel
Not one drop of oil left in the land.

Today you will say
As you leave on a light
Forget to turn off the TV
'It will be fine just this once'
Just this once.
Now imagine everyone
In every country in the world
Saying the same thing
Every day
Then maybe you'll think twice
When you take our world for granted.

Emma Donegan (14)
Lingfield Notre Dame Senior School, Lingfield

Extinction, Elimination, Eradication

On the floor lies a hollow husk, its life taken for merely a trifle,
Around it lie more, a dozen more trifles for the rich and pompous.
The evil wander away with their prizes, joking about the day's catch,
Their eyes wide and full of glee.
Another husk, more despair.
The huge mass of the fallen one bleeds from its great and brittle skin.
The malicious trundle away their vehicle laden with skin and flesh.
The ranks simply stand
Shoulder to shoulder
Back to back
Soul to soul.
The daily dose, the daily slumber.

Christopher Aris (14)
Lingfield Notre Dame Senior School, Lingfield

Why Do We?

Why do we do it?
Why do we feel the need to destroy others?
Why do we feel the need to take what's theirs?
Why do we suffocate the Earth?

Why is it?
Why is it that we waste what we possess?
Why is it that only a few of us feel the need to recycle?
Why is it we destroy what is a crucial part of our lives?

Why?

Why do we destroy our rainforests?

Laura Hookway (11)
Lingfield Notre Dame Senior School, Lingfield

How Can They Do Such A Thing?

Elephants are getting killed for it
When I'm sure we can live without it
How can they do such a thing?
Just how can they do such a thing? Poachers are its rival
Even though the elephants are fighting and fighting for their survival
Elephants' ivory catches their eye
That's all they want and they make them die.

Poachers love to grab them all right
Until they give the poor thing a fright
They get killed for just their skin
Their faces turn all sad and miserable
How can they do such a thing?
Just how can they do such a thing?
It's just not essential to the world
It's not needed that much and they make them suffer.

Another thing that gets killed for skin
It's such a beautiful animal
How could anyone have the nerve to even destroy it?
Imagine how gloomy they must be
Because they know their lives are going to be taken away
How can they do such a thing?
Just how can they do such a thing?
Zebras are what I am talking about.

Zeena Kerai (11)
Lingfield Notre Dame Senior School, Lingfield

What Have We Done?

What have we done to the world?
It's filling the air, the Earth, the sea, the sky
Poisoned, polluted the world.
What have we done?

Did you ever start to take notice?
Thieves we are
But why is it the elephant, seals are all
Demolished for their belongings?
What have we done?

Look what we've done!
All the plants, the protectors
We are tearing down, burning
All the preserves of human kind.
What have we done?

What about us?
Losing innocent loved ones
What about the promised peace
That you said for yours and mine?
What have we done to the world?
What have we done?

Trisha Nayee (11)
Lingfield Notre Dame Senior School, Lingfield

Pollution

Floating in the air we breathe
Unseen but there for sure
A cocktail full of chemicals
To kill before they cure

We help the mix with aerosols
To freshen, shine and paint
And wonder why we feel so ill
Or just a little faint

The residue from things we make
From factories flow to rivers
Diluted in our reservoirs
To pass through all our livers

Our bodies act like filters
Slowly filling up with waste
It's even in the food we eat
Put there to suit our taste

Before we had these things today
We had much less pollution
So if we banned them all right now
Could that be our solution?

Hamish Goff (12)
Lingfield Notre Dame Senior School, Lingfield

Waste

Pollution
It's bad for the world and kills off animals
What waste

Water
You fill up the bath to the top
What waste

Food
It stacks up on your plate
What waste

Electricity
It costs a lot and you leave it on
What waste

Friendship
If you fall out and don't make up
What waste.

Mackenzie Simpson (11)
Lingfield Notre Dame Senior School, Lingfield

A World Of Difference - Poems From The South

It's Going, Going . . .

As the bulldozers thrust and barge,
Torpedoing every tree in sight,
Without a thought, forests are going, going . . .

The elephant lies dead, surrounded by blood,
The poachers laugh at their own selfish greed,
Without a thought, elephants are going, going . . .

War planes swoop through the sky,
Devastation is scattered everywhere,
Without a thought, human life is going, going . . .

Watching as it trickles down the drain,
For others, it is like precious gold,
Without a thought, water is going, going . . .

Scrambling and shaking as the net traps them,
The fish cry as they are hauled aboard,
Without a thought, fish are going, going . . .

Slowly dying before our eyes,
Eventually there will be nothing left to save,
Without a thought, the world is going, going . . .
And it's gone.

Isabel Hazelton (11)
Lingfield Notre Dame Senior School, Lingfield

Just One More Tree

Plundering on, their heads held high,
An axe in one hand, down by their thigh.
Swinging destruction round past their shoulder,
For some of them a burden, like a heavy boulder.

Watching their homes being ruined one by one,
Listening to humans laughing, having fun.
More and more lives being lost every day,
Some species left with no one, no one to play.

Together Man could stop this,
Once and for all.
Stop endangering so much wildlife,
Stop endangering lives for all!

Emily Cornish (12)
Lingfield Notre Dame Senior School, Lingfield

Why?

What is it called
When your life has gone?
Maybe there's a way that we can talk,
To stop this world going into poverty and becoming lost.
The trees have gone, even though they're meant to stand tall,
The elephants' tusks are to be used,
But the elephant is now no use.
What was the point?
Forests are like ghost towns,
Fire still in the distance burning so strong.
War has broken out,
Where have the children gone?
Smoke pouring out of chimneys like the rain,
The sky crying out like a lost child.
Why have people done this?
Why has the Earth turned into a monster?
Why?

Maddy Groom (11)
Lingfield Notre Dame Senior School, Lingfield

Waste And Worry

War
Thousands of people are lost by this mass destruction and hate
Think

Pollution
Have you ever asked your mum to drive you somewhere when
It's really ten minutes' walk away?
Think

Rainforests
Thousands are killed during the process of cutting down trees
Think

Water
There are people dying in Africa from lack of water,
Hundreds a day
While we fill up a glass, take a sip and pour the rest away
Think

Fishing nets
Most dolphins and turtles die from fishing nets
When they've become tangled or trapped
Think

Extinction
All of the time, elephants and rhinos are being killed
For their tusks or hide
Think

If only we would look at what is happening around us
Things could change
Think.

Charlotte Hall (11)
Lingfield Notre Dame Senior School, Lingfield

What Have We Done To The World?

Listen to the birds
Living in the trees
Take one last look
At the world you hear.

What have we done
To the world?
What have we done?
You tell me.

See the elephant
By the waterhole
Then a few weeks later
See the ivory necklace in a shop.

What have we done
To the world?
What have we done?
You tell me.

Smell the resin of the trees
Then smell the wood in the air
See the tree fall
Soon to be firewood.

What have we done
To the world?
Can we stop this?
Can we rewind?

No, we can't
But we can try.

Thomas Corbett (11)
Lingfield Notre Dame Senior School, Lingfield

The World

The world is round,
It is a lovely place,
Nowhere is a better place to live than the world.

I love the fluffy white clouds like fluffy sheep in the sky,
The blazing orange sun warming your cold skin,
There is nothing warmer on your skin.

The grass is soft,
I could lie down in it for days.
Nowhere is more peaceful than the meadows.

The world is amazing.

It is destroyed by humans,
Pollution is making it horrible,
There is nothing worse to do than destroy the world.

Animals are extinct who once lived here,
Their homes have been destroyed,
Deforestation of the rainforests.

People die because of it,
Why doesn't anything happen to help?
Poverty.

It is horrible.

Why?

Edward Willment (12)
Lingfield Notre Dame Senior School, Lingfield

The Earth's Death

Smoky air,
Cloudy space,
Why is Earth a dirty place?

The Earth is a special place,
It carries the entire human race,
So don't disgrace it,
Save it!

Who did this?
Was it you?
It's pollution roaming through.

Running free,
Through the air,
Litter everywhere, no one cares.

You don't ever
Think each day
About the world, it disintegrates.

Think a little deeper,
Once in a while,
The fact will *never* make you smile.

Demi Barnes (11)
Lingfield Notre Dame Senior School, Lingfield

A World Of Difference - Poems From The South

Can We Stop It Now?

Can we stop war and death?
Can we stop pollution and deforestation?
Can we fix all our mistakes?
Or should we just give up
And leave our mess for others to clear up?
No!
We can stop it now,
It's now or never.
Think of all the children who die in wars,
Think of all the animals hunted down for money,
Think of the pollution and the grief it has caused us.
Our world is like a chance you get once and then it's over.
If we don't take that chance now, we may never get another one.
Can you imagine the world without animals and trees,
Or food and water?
There would be no world for us to wreck,
If we don't stop it now.
Can we stop it now?
Have we come too far?
Is the world destroyed beyond repair
Or can we solve our problem
By recycling, not cutting down trees, stopping animal hunting
And restoring peace to the world?
We can help the world last longer
By each doing our little bit.

Alice Clutterbuck (12)
Lingfield Notre Dame Senior School, Lingfield

Wars

Wars - heartbreaking
Why do we have them?
Why? Why? Why?
Do the politicians think about what they're doing?
The people lose their loved ones
Wars ruin our world
They damage homes, buildings and lives
Do the people causing it care?
Do they know what they are doing?
When they fire a gun, do they stop to think?
No!
They just carry on shooting, shooting, shooting
When they drop a bomb
Do they think about the people they are going to kill?
No!
When they come charging in on their trucks
Do they think about the people they're frightening?
No!
Give peace a chance!

Madison Cahill-Smith (11)
Lingfield Notre Dame Senior School, Lingfield

Is It Fair?

Is it fair that children die,
When the answer is so clear?
Why do animals have to be killed
When the answer is right here?

Cruelly killed for their tusks,
The elephant lies down to sleep.
Children who are lost in war,
Their mothers can only weep.

The slow groan of the trees,
They seem to fall so fast.
Coughing as the smoke descends,
Let's hope it will not last.

Animals are dying.
Can you help?
People are crying.
Can you help?

Shannon Bridger (12)
Lingfield Notre Dame Senior School, Lingfield

Where Would We Be?

Where would we be,
Without birdsong in the morning?
Without eves of sunlight dawning?
Where would we be without all these trivial pleasures?
If we don't take measures,
Where would we be?

Where would we be,
Without towering forests in all their glory?
Without all the scent of woods, pine, wollemi and redwood,
Each one telling a story?
Where would we be without these?
We'd have little air left to breathe even a sigh of relief.
Where would we be?

Where would we be,
Without animals, just thinking of our own lives to pander?
Without thinking about creatures dear, as the wolf and panda?
Where would we be with no life but us on Earth?
Loneliness etched all over its girth.
Where would we be?

Where would we be,
Without frozen blankets of snow and just the blistering heat?
Without the cool water springs, just burns on our feet?
Where would we be, without April blooms in the spring
And jazzy autumn leaves?
That's something alone no man could retrieve.
Where would we be?

Where would we be,
Without children playing in the street?
Without houses standing guard watchfully, grand and serene?
Where would we be if war tore us apart,
So one day we're here, the next we're not?
Silence ringing through a once joyous town, everybody just left to rot.
Where would we be?

The message now is: *where would you be?*

Emily Bassett (11)
Lingfield Notre Dame Senior School, Lingfield

Pollution Solution

'So now I guess you're gonna say,
That the factories caused all this dismay.'
'Yes I am and it is true,
And cars polluted the air too!'

'I don't believe you, but I might,
How do you know what you see is right?'
'Don't you see? It's all around you,
Now there are several things we *can* do.'

'So are the things in the air that fly,
Also causing the Earth to die?'
'I don't know. Do you mean planes?
Yes, they cause a lot of pain!'

'So are there many things we can do?
I can only think of a few.
'There are several, here's a few,
Now just hold on a second or two.'

'Yes, I'm listening, tell me now!
I really want to learn how!'
'Well, for starters, walk most places,
Don't use cars, to save Earth's faces!'

'OK then, that's what I'll do,
Nothing else for now, thank you.'
'You're very welcome, you are so right,
Little steps at a time, that's right!'

Jessica Dickins (12)
Lingfield Notre Dame Senior School, Lingfield

Black And White

We are just the same,
We may not look alike
But we share the same pain.

When I walk into the classroom
It should not be,
That everyone looks at me.

We live and dream
We love and hate
We're all the same
And we share the same fate.

Beata Borelius-Larson (12)
Notre Dame Senior School, Cobham

Day By Day

I sit there day by day
With nothing to look at.
The colours black and grey
Make no happiness.

I sit there day by day
With nothing to hear.
If only the trees would sway,
There is no happiness.

I sit there day by day
Nothing to see or hear.
The world is poisoned, you have to pray,
There's no colour, happiness, no life.

Joanna Simpson (12)
Notre Dame Senior School, Cobham

Rubbish

R emember to clean up your mess and recycle,
U se your bins and keep the lid on,
B ecause otherwise the animals destroy it,
B lue bins, green bins, black bins,
whatever the colour put litter in them,
I am very concerned, so you should put your mess in the bin,
S hould you not have a bin near you then put it in your bag
and keep it till you're near one,
H edgehogs are one of the animals that can be affected
if you don't put your rubbish in the bin,so remember to
put it in the bin!

Alex Adams (12)
Notre Dame Senior School, Cobham

Climate Change

Can't we see,
What could be,
Look at the world around us.

Dusty air,
We don't even care,
Dirty seas,
Not enough trees.

We're being mean,
By not being clean
And becoming so lazy.

Yes, we're having progress
But we're forgetting the world around us.

Charlotte Robeson (12)
Notre Dame Senior School, Cobham

Untitled

The world was a beautiful place,
It should be adored by every face.
But now it's grubby; rubbish, landfills, sadness.

Unless we open our eyes
To what is in front of us.
Destroyed rivers and lakes.
By doing small things
We can make a big difference.
Pick up that crisp packet,
Recycle that bottle,
Make a difference.

Alexandra Lee Harvey (13)
Notre Dame Senior School, Cobham

Ocean

The ocean, crystal clear and blue,
Almost perfect, as good as new,
Then later you will see,
That the ocean is a home for you and me.
Poisoned and destroyed,
Ruining the beautiful view and making us annoyed,
Pumping all these chemicals into the sea,
It will soon be gone and we will not see
The ocean as a home for us,
Welcoming us with open arms.

Gloria Nyangiye (12)
Notre Dame Senior School, Cobham

A World Of Difference - Poems From The South

Save The Cold Climate

To keep Alaska white and the Northern Lights bright
You have to turn off your unnecessary light,

Recycle all your cardboard
Then all the polar bears will be reassured,

Use your blue bins
For paper, card and tins.

Now you all know how to behave
Come on, we've got a planet to save!

Lucy Walters (11)
Notre Dame Senior School, Cobham

Legs!

We have these things called legs,
They hang from our hips like pegs.
We use these odd things to walk,
Not to sit in a car and talk.
We want to be green,
Now let's not be mean.
Now use these odd things to walk!
If you wanna be green,
You've gotta be keen,
To keep going, to keep walking,
Not to sit down and start talking!
Help us be keen,
We'll show you the *Big Green Poetry Machine!*

Tilly Prowse (11)
Notre Dame Senior School, Cobham

Save The Animals

H elp save the animals of our Earth.
E nsure that our children see a tiger or a polar bear.
L et all of the species survive.
P lease help the Earth as it has helped us.

T he destruction of the rainforest has made their homes smaller.
H elp to recycle to save our Earth's resources.
E nable us all to recycle so our Earth can live on.

A nimals eat litter because they think it's food, then they die.
N ot everyone recycles. Do you?
I t's humans destroying the ozone layer.
M elting ice caps means less land to live on.
A ll animals have the right to live so why are we killing them?
L ike us, animals need homes.
S ave the world's animals.

Olivia Astles (11)
Notre Dame Senior School, Cobham

We Have To Take Action Now!

Do you want to live in a smoke-fumed world?
If I said yes that would be a lie,
So we have to take action now and this is why . . .
Put all your rubbish in a bin
So don't go cutting off the fishes' fins.
It's no fun when the world passes by,
Not when you see children cry,
So we have to take action and that is no lie!
Wash in and drink less water
I also don't agree with animal slaughter
Us humans are wasting the planet
Like watching TV, we should ban it!
We have to take action now and this is no lie!

Isabelle Stewart (12)
Notre Dame Senior School, Cobham

The Big Green Poem

The sky so clear,
Global warming so mere,
The trees and animals so healthy,
The people so wealthy,
The streets so clean.
What a wonderful world this would be!
The air is cloudy,
Everyone feels drowsy,
All living things are thin,
Our future is grim,
The trees have no leaves,
What a spiteful world this would be!

Melina Klein (11)
Notre Dame Senior School, Cobham

It's No Joke

It's not a joke anymore.
It's not a joke about the rain that pours.
It's not a joke about the sky of black
Because all I want, is the blue sky back.

It's not a joke anymore.
It's not a joke the way people die.
It's not a joke the way children cry
Because all I want, is for you to try.

It's not a joke anymore.
It's not a joke the way bullets soar.
It's not a joke the way bombs blow
Because all I want, is for the nations to grow.

Now it's time to hold hands,
Across the many, many lands.
As people start to share
And as people start to care.

It's no joke.
We must take action *now*.

Sarah Shutt (11)
Notre Dame Senior School, Cobham

Future Through The Eyes Of A Soldier

Time will tell,
Time will tell,
When the battlefield ends,
The shot of the barrel disappears into the horizon.
Just like our world will one day.
We have lent our world into the unsure hands of science.

Although the world is thrown askew,
I think it will keep on living,
That is if we take care.
Now.

Isabelle Cook (11)
Notre Dame Senior School, Cobham

My Litter Haikus

Shapes fluttering high,
Is this litter in the sky?
What are we to do?

The world's polluted,
We need to recycle now
Before it's too late!

Do it now!

Natasha Williams (11)
Notre Dame Senior School, Cobham

Let's Imagine . . .

Let's imagine . . .

Imagine a world without pandas.
Their thick fur and giant paws.
Without them would be like a face without a smile.

Imagine the desert without meerkats.
Their bobbing heads and stripy backs.
Without them would be like a garden without flowers.

Imagine the Arctic without penguins.
Their pointed beaks and black and white skin.
Without them would be like a night without stars.

Imagine the plains without cheetahs.
Their striking coats and incredible speed.
Without them would be like a river without fish.

As the sun goes down another of these beautiful creatures will disappear.

Allegra Gordon (11)
Notre Dame Senior School, Cobham

Let's Walk It!

We wake up late.
You'll never get to school at this rate.
You throw your clothes on.
Say, 'Dad get a move on!'
You jump in the car.
It's not that far.
Why use it?
I think I'll walk it!
It's helping the planet and the traffic's manic.
So why not walk it!

Imogen Alexandra Boffin (11)
Notre Dame Senior School, Cobham

The Rainforest

The rainforest is a place where the animals live
The monkeys swing from branch to branch
Whilst the fish swim in the river.

But there are less branches now for the monkeys to swing on
The rivers are becoming polluted,
This is all because of us.
We are cutting down the trees
We are polluting the rivers.

You can help put a stop to this
You can recycle or reuse your paper and rubbish
Walk or ride a bike instead of using a car.

If you do your bit to help save the planet
We will live in a better place.
We will see the monkeys swing from branch to branch
And the fish swim in the rivers.

Rachel Bertie (11)
Notre Dame Senior School, Cobham

Be Green

G o out and be green!
R euse, recycle
E nvironment is crying!
E cology is trying!
N o more rubbish.

Charley James (11)
Notre Dame Senior School, Cobham

Save The Animals

Another species fades away,
Will this destruction never end?
How many animals must die
To satisfy the human race?
Does no one know? Does no one care?
Can no one hear their dying cries?
It's all our fault! We're killing off
Our animal friends, big and small
Their homes are disappearing fast
Their forests falling to the ground
Their oceans filled with trash and oil
Our poisons fill their cleaner air.
We'll ask ourselves *where did they go*
Those animals we used to know?
No one will know, no one will care.
Our fires still smoke, our cars still blare.
But we can help! Let's help them now!
Let's share the Earth and keep it clean,
Let's come together as a team
To help the animals,
We'll all go green and not be mean
And save the animals!

Lorna Hughes (11)
Notre Dame Senior School, Cobham

Global Warming

Throw your litter away,
Animals are getting killed,
Humans bring destruction.

Icebergs are melting,
Animals are getting killed,
Humans bring destruction.

It's getting warmer,
Animals are getting killed,
Humans bring destruction.

Sasha Kennington (11)
Prior's Field School, Godalming

The Rainforest

In the rainforest,
Trees fall down all around us.
Please help to save them.
Recycle cardboard,
plastic, paper, glass.
Please help to save them.
Cycle to places.
Driving can pollute the world.
Please save them.

Emma Kendall (11)
Prior's Field School, Godalming

Save Our World

S ave our world
A nd all the animals too
V isit the real world
E skimos and polar bears will go.

O ur world will go
U can help
R ushing and ignoring will not do anything.

W ith everyone joining in
O ur world will survive
R ecycling can make a difference
L oving and caring
D o it, and we will all be happy!

Holly Morganti (11)
Prior's Field School, Godalming

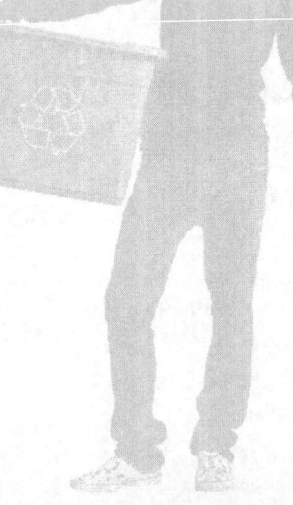

Eco-Friendly

E verybody could help by many different ways.
   The question is would they?
C an people really help the world by recycling and reducing pollution?
O nly humans can help global warming, because think about it,
   animals can't, can they?
F orever if no one does anything, then the world will have no
   chance of surviving, will it?
R ighteousness is what humans need. If no one does anything then
   in generations on, what will happen to them?
I gnorant are the majority of selfish people who cannot be bothered
   to help the world. Do you think that?
E nvironmental schools are a great example to the world.
   Why aren't all schools like that?
N ever think that not helping won't make a difference. You can ask
   anyone and guess what the answer will be?
D enying the fact that there will be a bad ending, is never the way to go.
L aughing about it is what kids do, but in fifty years time it will be no joke.
Y es you may read this poem and be confused, but this is no joke.
   The environment is dying and it needs your help.

Harriet Thacker (11)
Prior's Field School, Godalming

Differences

Look at the people on the street,
And doesn't it make you wonder,
What would it be like to meet
Someone from Down Under?

Look at the people with riches and fame,
That wanted to help but just couldn't
Some just always act the play,
But then they just wouldn't.

Look at the differences we have today,
And then look at them tomorrow,
You wouldn't really want to say,
Just some of the horrors.

Some people suffer every day,
Some just try . . .
Some people want to stay,
But just walk on by.

Sophie Jane Evans (11)
Prior's Field School, Godalming

Our World

Our world now has a lot of pollution,
Now we have to find a solution.

Recycling can help our planet stay fresh,
By reusing the stuff that makes a mess.

Litter is dangerous if left on the ground,
Causing injury to animals if not found.

Cutting down trees is bad for the air,
Replanting the trees shows that we care.

We can help by changing our ways,
So our future children have brighter days.

Charlotte Hardy (11)
Prior's Field School, Godalming

A World Of Difference - Poems From The South

Life Or No Life?

You have lived, you live, you will live.
But for how much longer?
I will try to help you.
Whenever you hear me, you do not wish to listen to me.
You try to betray me.
When I talk I release love, but you ignore me.
If feel like you want to kill me.
I will die one day.
You won't care, you'll die as well.

Alexandra Paule (11)
Prior's Field School, Godalming

Homeless

H opeless without a home describes our miserable lives.
O ut by ourselves without the security of shelter.
M y body is cold, we all wish for some warmth.
E verywhere I look, homes lie in tatters.
L iving was once fun, full of joy and comfort, then
E vil arrived, dressed in the coat of a storm.
S ilently, shuffling and shuddering it came with
S inister strength, the rain held hands with the wicked wind,
                                    spreading a tangle of terror.

Kelly McCall (12)
Prior's Field School, Godalming

YoungWriters

Cheetah's View

Every day I look out over the grasslands,
As the sun rises, my spirits do.
I watch a meerkat stand,
Do you know who I am, do you?

I am a noble cat, a proud cat,
I stalk with stealth and heed.
I hunt whilst little birds chat,
And I ambush the prey for food I need.

I am not around much more,
I am endangered you see.
Some of you live on the British shore,
What could you do to help me?

Well, you could not use a car but take the bus,
Recycle your plastic, paper and glass.
Everything you do could help every one of us,
Please let us show some class.

Turn off your light when you leave a room,
Turn off the tap when you brush your teeth.
Use less petrol in your cars, *vroom!*
Pick up litter which you see on the heath!

The ice caps are melting fast,
Pandas are hunted too.
Whales are less in the ocean vast,
Do you know what to do?

Do your best to help the world,
Be *green* my friends, be *green*,
So we animals can sleep soundly and tightly curled,
Don't be mean, don't be mean.

Help us for the good of the world!

Rebecca West (12)
Prior's Field School, Godalming

Untitled

I am the thing which is causing a huff,
I am like a wall which separates a child from a father.
Which separates a wife from a husband.
I don't care if you're rich or poor, young or old.
I hurt you anyway.
Stop before it's out of control.
I am one of the things which is bad in this world.
I am something that is life or death.
What am I?
I am war.
Do anything you can to stop me.
To make this world a better place.
Stop before we all perish.

Maddie Demaine (11)
Prior's Field School, Godalming

The Earth Is Warming

Young birds chirp to the rise of the early morning sun,
Trees breathe in the wind as the lungs of the world.
The Earth is living.

The cities awake as busy cars rush to and fro,
Energy that takes millennia to form, takes minutes to burn.
The Earth is warming.

Innocent animals feed on litter to live, only to die,
Factories exhale fumes like a million chain smokers,
The Earth is sickening.

Jet planes soar, burning invisible holes in the sky,
Icebergs tumble to the sea; tragic, like the Titanic.
The Earth is vanishing.

Tidal waves rage, swallowing up the land,
The world is still, as it takes its final breath.
The Earth is dead.

Lucy Stocks (11)
Prior's Field School, Godalming

I Wished I Were . . .

I wished I were a dinosaur,
Pink, purple and green,
But then I changed my mind,
As they could not be seen.

I wished I were a mammoth,
To live until my teens,
But then I changed my mind,
As they could not be seen.

I wished I were a dog,
Not big, ferocious or mean,
But then I realised,
They too will not be seen.

I wish I wasn't human,
I'm big, ferocious and mean,
But I soon
Will not be seen.

So when you next throw away
Think, be green,
Or you too will not be seen.

Eleanor Lunt (11)
Prior's Field School, Godalming

Planet Earth

The Earth used to be calmer
The people used to be calmer
The people had no worries
The people had not one quarry

The heat on Earth is expanding
The forest fires are starting
The Earth is filled with litter
The atmosphere is bitter

The harmony has blown away
I only have one thing to say
Blow away the Earth's misery
Please read this list to save

Please try not to drive a car
Please plant some trees in your garden
Please recycle your food and waste
By putting it in the compost bin

Thank you, thank you for listening
To my important list
This would be good to use today
The planet needs your help.

Anna Sligo-Young (11)
Prior's Field School, Godalming

Earth

You don't know who I am,
But you will soon.

I am the one that destroys your houses,
I am the one that floods your homes.

I am the one that's in your heart,
I am the one that's all alone.

I am the one you worry about,
I am the one that makes you shout.

I am the one who loves you dearly,
I am the one.

You live on me,
You care for me,
You say that I'm amazing.

I am the one
Who is your
Earth,
I am the one.

Yolanda Foo (11)
Prior's Field School, Godalming

The Earth

I am Space, almighty and great,
I love all my planets but one,
I'm ashamed of its people,
They make it too hot,
They have just got it all wrong.
They are bullying themselves and getting no rest,
They are polluting the seas and killing the best,
They are wasting the fuels and cutting down trees,
All the animals are dying, especially the bees.
What is the name of this planet so small?
The Earth is the answer to my riddle so cool.

Lydia Jarvis (11)
Prior's Field School, Godalming

Half The World

Half the world lives,
Half the world makes,
Half the world gives
While the other half takes.

Half the world hates,
Half the world runs away,
Half the world's late,
Half the world praises the day.

Half the world is,
Half the world was,
Half the world thinks,
Half the world does.

Half the world lies,
Half the world burns,
Half the world cries
While the other half turns.

Half the world cares,
Half the world weeps,
Half the world shares,
Half the world keeps.

Half the world sings,
Half the world laughs,
Half the world brings.

Nicole Harper (12)
Prior's Field School, Godalming

O Green World

As I walk through the dark and gloomy forest,
The trees communicate with me,
I see the birth of a new life, shattered by our revolution,
I'm shown the relatives of these trees, shredded to mere dust.
They guide me to the elders from before time began,
And allow me to see the world before mine, when the trees
And humans lived in harmony.
'Once,' they say, 'the world was just green.
Not red, not purple, not blue, but green.
All around the campfires they'd chant, 'O green world!'
Through the forest we'd hum, 'O green world!'
It is our only hope, our only chance,
And our final wish is that the world be green again.'

Holly James (11)
Prior's Field School, Godalming

Pollution

Pollution is a terrible thing,
The world is about to ping,
There is a solution,
To stop the pollution,
People should open their eyes,
To find a big surprise,
Don't let it get worse,
The ozone is about to burst!

Alex Lucy (11)
Prior's Field School, Godalming

A Life

I live as a polar bear in the melting land of the Arctic.
I live as a monkey in the high trees crashing down.
I live as a tiger in the hot land of India, buy my fur might soon be gone.
I live as a gorilla in the bamboo forests; people hunt me and I don't know why.
I live as a three-toed sloth; I get hunted for my toes, they are lucky but not for me.
I live as everything; the animals, the land, the Earth!

Seeing is believing.

Abbey Prichard (11)
Prior's Field School, Godalming

Love The Earth

When I was young, I was green and new.
I was covered in dinosaurs of every hue.
A meteor hit me in the nose
And all the dinosaurs went away.
Then it was winter and the Ice Age came.

I'm now covered in these things called humans,
They are making a terrible mess, burning my old friends for fuel.

I feel hot and sick and have a real pain in my ozone.
My caps are beginning to melt, please send help.

Love,
The Earth.

Samantha Sutton (11)
Prior's Field School, Godalming

Can Earth Be Earth

Can Earth be Earth when the seas are gone?
Can trees shine green?
And can skies be sky when the sun has moved on?
Can the sun be seen?

Soon our Earth will be gone
And the shining skies too.
There will be nothing to live on,
What shall we do?

Do you want people's lives to be like this
With the skies dark and grey
Or do you want them living in bliss?
If you do then you have to act today!

Miema Baker (12)
Prior's Field School, Godalming

The Sea's Plea

Waves - the way the white horses break on the shore, through storm and calm.
Tides - when the sea goes out it has had enough pollution, when it comes in it is trying again, giving you another chance.
Colours - blue and magically glistening in the sun.
Life - the sea is full of it, from big to small, in every corner you will find life.
Light and shade - at the deepest points in the seas it is the darkest but above them it is at the brightest and clearest.
Fish to feed our hunger - fishing for more and more fish, but we are running out . . . dying out . . . gone.
Wasted life - we are wasting all the precious life, you can't get the life back, what have we done?
Oil - thick, black, sticky blobs sucking the life out of the sea like bloodthirsty leeches.
Bags - the floating manmade jellyfish, which is working alongside with bloodthirsty leeches.
Choking - the bags and the oil are choking the sea, soon it will be gone and left in its place will be a Sahara desert which will go on forever looking for a drop of water which used to cover the ground.

Sophie Field (12)
Prior's Field School, Godalming

The Tree

The axe punctured the tough skin of the muscular body,
Again and again it struck the tree until it could put up a fight no longer.
Slowly, slowly it came down;
The anchors split unwillingly,
They screamed for help, for mercy, for life.
Crash!
It hit the ground,
The noise echoed everywhere,
But there was nobody around, nobody around to listen to the sorrowful cries;
nobody around to care.
But I was there.
I heard the pleas of the dying tree.
I cared.
But what is one person who cares to a world that is killing itself?
Nothing . . .
I am nothing . . .

Molly D'Angelo (12)
Prior's Field School, Godalming

Destroying Our World

What about now?
What about today?
What if we're making it all that it's meant to be?
What about our homes?
Where do we stand?
It's bubbling up inside, ready to burst,
Holding it in, all for our sakes.
Respecting us,
Doing its best.
We're destroying the world,
But we're hurting ourselves.

Emily Milton (12)
Prior's Field School, Godalming

Recycling

The eyes of the creatures that live in the sea,
They swim and swim until they find me,
They plead and plead and jump and yelp,
They scratch, they scream and cry for help.

The plastic and smoke fills our lungs,
The oil and fumes coat our tongues,
The glass and metal stab our eyes,
Sharp edges just like knives
Pierce through our tender thighs.

Litter floats in the atmosphere,
Falling into the empty chair,
The stream collects the metal rust
And absorbs the polluted dust,
Until the Earth is just a crust.

I look, I look into the skies,
The dreams, the dreams that once lit our eyes,
What have we done?
What shall we do?
It's all down to me and you.

Ellen Bryden (12)
Prior's Field School, Godalming

A Little Less Conversation And A Little More Action!

As I sit here in this mess,
I begin to wonder,
Has this world lost its mind?
When I used to smell the fresh air
Now all I smell is regret!

I used to hear the cry of the wild animals,
Now all I hear is poverty crying dirty tears
Of hunger, illness and death,
Why?

I used to believe that this world was beautiful,
A creation of Mother Nature,
An untouched beauty,
Now I know what this world has become!

Look what we've done,
Look at this world only crying out for one!
Look, how could this have become this spinning
World of tears, pain and sorrow?

Now I sit here and think
Look at this world,
We know what we can do,
Put your foot down
And turn this world around.
Understand this place,
We are turning it from *green* to *blue*.

So just one thing I want is a little less conversation
And a little more action,
You know what we have to do!

Genevieve Labuschagne (12)
Prior's Field School, Godalming

Earth Is Ending?

Look at the Earth,
It looks different, horrible,
Why did we do it?
Why don't we care?
Look at the trees around us,
All cluttered up with plastic bags,
Our food is covered in plastic,
Why can't it be in paper bags?
The world is changing rapidly,
And it's all because of us,
Why can't we leave it alone
And let it have a future?
The sea is turning into oil
Ruining all the fish.
We can change,
But we can't be bothered,
It's going to go, end,
You know it is,
So does everyone,
So what do we choose?
What path do we take?
Can we reverse this deadly mistake?
Why don't we try?
The way we're going,
We're all going to die.

Jemima Sexton (12)
Prior's Field School, Godalming

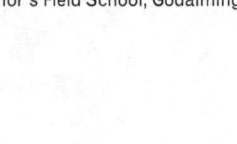

What Have We Done?

Why have we done this?
Look what we've done.
Look at the weeping skies
And the blazing sun.

What are these promises?
What do they mean?
All has been said
But nothing has been seen.

Things have to change,
Really they do!
We need to work together
Or the Earth will turn to . . .

I believe we can do it!
Make it a better place,
All we need is effort,
Don't lose face!

Evangeline Clery (12)
Prior's Field School, Godalming

Gone

It's gone,
Everything is gone.
The trees smothered in plastic bags and poisoned,
Uprooted and made into something new.

The animals . . . gone.
Polar bears, birds, horses, lions, leopards, elephants, giraffes.
What have we done?
We have slaughtered them, destroyed their homes,
Poisoned them, eaten them or worn their skins.

We are murderers of what used to be a wonderful planet.
If only we had done something.
We could have changed everything
If only we had talked less and done more,
But we can't now,
It is gone.

Ella Carey (12)
Prior's Field School, Godalming

Why Should I Care?

Why should I care about global warming?
It doesn't affect me after all.
All my mates say I'm ignoring
But what can I do?

Why should I care about global warming?
It doesn't affect me after all.
The world won't end in my lifetime,
So what should I do?

Why should I care about global warming?
People say the world will flood
But I don't live near water
So why should I care?

Why should I care about global warming?
I like the smell of polluted air,
I like seeing people die of hunger,
It doesn't affect me after all.

As I sit here now, the clouds crying, the sun blazing,
Waters flooding, litter everywhere, the smell of smoke in the air
And people crying,
I wonder why I didn't care,
It affected me after all . . .

Susannah Whitmarsh (13)
Prior's Field School, Godalming

What Can I Do?

The Earth is crying, dying.
Calling out, warning us, telling us to stop.
Stop doing what?
Every wave that laps up onto the sand is whispering, 'Help, help, help.'
Every leaf on every tree is whimpering, 'Why? Why? Why?'
We are killing our Earth,
Killing the world we live in, killing our home.

The rainforests are being cut for us.
We live, they die.
The animals die and we live.
Since when were we the most important creatures?
We have power, so we use it against our own home, our own creatures.

Every tree is like a zebra, swaying their tails along with the rhythm of the wind,
And we, we are the lions, stalking the zebras, waiting for the moment to strike.
We kill them, eat them, leave them.
Why?

Cars put out carbon dioxide, choking our Earth, making it unable to breathe.
We're choking the life out of our own home!
The Earth is drowning in the emissions our machines put out,
Drowning in a sea of carbon dioxide.

What can I do? What difference can I make?
I'm only one fish in the ocean of life.
I'm only one, you're only one, we're only one,
But together, we're everyone.

Julia Parison (12)
Prior's Field School, Godalming

Rainforests

R ainforests are dying, being stabbed by saws and sliced by machines.
A nimals are suffering, like abused children.
I mportant people power over them, like a lion in front of some mice.
N ever has a problem to stop the catastrophes come true.
F ish are stones, dropping one by one to the dusty, murky floors of rivers.
O n land and offshore, our forests are dying.
R ivers choked with dead fish and pieces of sad, broken trees.
E very person living there, crying for help, like poor starving children.
S tories of tragedy being told worldwide.
T rees are being slaughtered like chickens on a battery farm.
S top destroying our rainforests forever!

Kimi Worsdell (12)
Prior's Field School, Godalming

The River Keeps Crying

The river keeps crying
As we make things for ourselves,
The river keeps suffering
As it flows miserably down the country.

The river keeps crying
As we pump death into its tears,
The river keeps weeping
As its blue body turns to black.

The river keeps crying
As Man ignores its plight,
The river keeps howling
As it begins to dry out.

The river keeps crying
As life begins to drift away,
The river stops crying
Everyone too busy to notice its death.

Harriet Martin (12)
Prior's Field School, Godalming

But Why?

The sea . . . drowning with pollution . . .
The rainforest . . . slaughtered with scraps . . .
The animals . . . strangled with rubbish . . .
But why? Because of us.

> The beaches . . . stoned in packets . . .
> The grass . . . smothered in junk . . .
> The world . . . strangled with rubbish . . .
> But why? Because of us.

>> So . . . think before you act . . .
>> So . . . recycle every day . . .
>> So we can make a difference . . .
>> But why? Because we can change . . .

Ella Briscoe & Rebeccah Webber (12)
Prior's Field School, Godalming

Welcome To Nature

Welcome to nature, human style.
We killed the forests and the animals' habitats.
I open the window and see a beautiful meadow full of . . .
Tin can flowers,
Plastic bag trees,
Cigarette grass,
Bushes of bottles,
Dead animals lie around us because of us.
Where will it end?
With us!

Katherine Oliver (12)
Prior's Field School, Godalming

The Plastic Bag Tree

The plastic bag tree was
Out of breath, finding it hard to breathe,
All the bags still didn't leave.
Entangled in the tree's spine,
Still not letting go after nine.

Over and over the cars went past the tree,
Not letting the old thing be.
It breathes in polluted air,
Everyone should really care
About the plastic bag tree.

No one else is to blame,
We have all the shame,
Of letting this tree die!

Charlotte Sullivan (13)
Prior's Field School, Godalming

From The Factory's Depths

Puffing from the darkness
Out comes the smoke
Letting loose destruction
Upon the humans who choke.

Fumes are letting loose
So you'd better watch out
We're coming to destroy you
And your cosy couch.

Swirling through the sky
Fogging up their world
Strangling the crops
Hurting the animals.

Sarah Quinton (12)
Prior's Field School, Godalming

The Earth - Haikus

The world is dying,
We are all to blame for it,
Stop the madness now!

You should never kill,
Well, you are killing a lot,
You should be ashamed.

Stop! Recycle now.
Stop! Be kind to the Earth now!
Stop! Now start helping.

Millie McKee (11)
Prior's Field School, Godalming

Our Green World - Haikus

Animals slip through
Because the ice is melting,
Please stop using cars.

Cars make pollution
Which causes global warming,
We have to stop this.

We can walk instead,
Even cycle on your bike,
You could use the bus!

Recycle paper,
The rainforests are cut down,
But you can save them ...

The world is quite green,
Though we can make it greener,
Please save our planet.

Charlotte Goodfellow (11)
Prior's Field School, Godalming

I Wonder

Looking out a window, staring into space,
Not really paying attention in maths,
I wondered what life would be like as an iceberg,
Slowly melting away, descending while polar bears pounce on you.
Life is so short.
Life is so dull.
I wonder how many minutes until I have melted completely.
Blank, dead already, I thought, *let's think of something else.*
I wondered what life would be like as a pheasant.
If I were a pheasant I would fly around in the smoky sky,
Dodging the bullets.
Bang! Dead already I thought.
Life is so short. Let's make the world better.

Chesca Loggia (11)
Prior's Field School, Godalming

Tree - Haiku

Why do they do this?
We have feelings too you know,
One cut and blackness.

Alice Budge (11)
Prior's Field School, Godalming

A Bird's Plea

I am who I am,
I am my food,
I am my home,
But when they come
They ruin my food,
They ruin my home,
Why do they come?

Anna Hudson (11)
Prior's Field School, Godalming

Haikus

Polluting my world
Clouds of thick black smoke,
Bellowing out of chimneys,
Polluting my world.

Clubbed
Why do they hurt us?
Hitting us over the head,
Then taking us home.

Why?
Stepping in litter
It is very disgusting,
Why do we do it?

Farrell Cranstone (12)
Prior's Field School, Godalming

Untitled

More and more have longer to swim to return home each day.
The longer they swim, the more tired they get
And more of them pass away.
Climate change is affecting us all,
But not as much as the polar bear.
The ice is melting, the water's rising,
So don't leave on lights, don't dare!
These creatures are endangered,
So don't let us become
The last ones to remember them,
We'd be the only ones.
Switch off, walk and save lives!

Melissa Price (12)
Prior's Field School, Godalming

Life

All the endangered animals
Playing in the trees,
Along comes a bulldozer,
Where are the monkeys?

All the little animals
Being clubbed to death,
All because a man
Wants a warm chest.

Cruelty to animals
Is really unfair,
But one day it will turn around
And along comes a bear.

Leave the animals alone,
Give them a home,
I'm begging you please,
Don't kill the monkeys.

Emma Droutis (12)
Prior's Field School, Godalming

Homeless

I live on my own.
I have nowhere to go.
I have no home.
I am all alone.

I live in an alleyway.
I live on a doorstep.
I live in a dustbin.
I live without a home.
I have no clothes, I sit around and mope.
I am starving to death
And I have no hope.

Amy Crawford (12)
Prior's Field School, Godalming

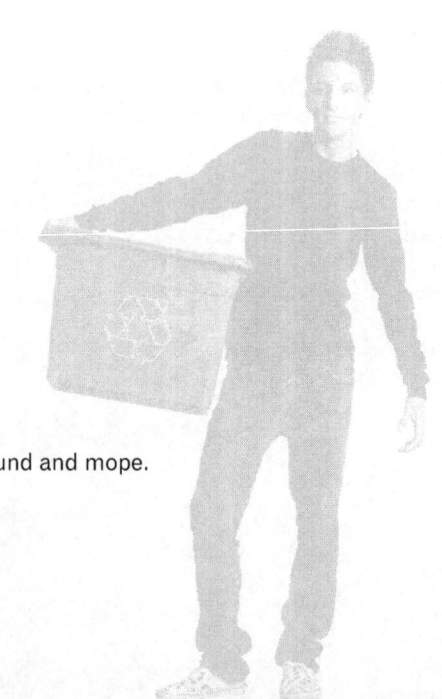

Destruction

I gave you a rainforest,
You destroyed it.
I gave you a countryside,
You destroyed it.
I gave you a beach,
You destroyed it.

You sent droughts to Africa
And people ran out of food.
You sent floods to China
And people lost their homes.
You sent storms to Asia
And people died.

I gave you a clean environment,
You polluted it.
Most of all I gave you a chance
You took advantage of it.

Lois King (12)
Prior's Field School, Godalming

In Tune With Mother Nature

If you listen to the songbirds as they greet the summer sun
And love the way the wind can make the trees sing just for fun.

If you like to hear the ocean as it drums upon the shore
And imagine all the waves out there and hope they'll sing some more.

If you think of all the animals as players in a band,
Each with a lovely tune to play, all needed on the land.

If you honour every little thing as a part of nature's treasure,
You're in tune with Mother Nature so let's all sing her song together.

Hanna Stephen (12)
Prior's Field School, Godalming

Hypocrite

Would you like it if I came in and destroyed your house
With a saw, one that has teeth and an evil laugh?
You wouldn't like it if I destroyed your house.

So then, why? Why, do you chop the monkey's house down
With a saw that has teeth and an evil laugh?
Because you wouldn't like it if I destroyed your house.

If I destroyed your house you would live on the streets,
Uncomfortable, and with nothing to eat.
You would be sad and have to find a new home,
So you wouldn't like it if I destroyed your house.

So then, why? Why do you chop the monkey's house down?
He now lives on the floor with nowhere to sleep and nowhere to snore.
He is now sad and has to find a new home,
Because he doesn't like it when you chop his house down.

Kate Alexander (12)
Prior's Field School, Godalming

Earth

With climate change and global warming
Pollution is rising but rainforests are falling.

The Earth's poor state is not really great
But what we could do is, create a better place.

Recycle your paper, your pots and your tops,
Or even take them to charity shops.

Whether it's new or old or good or bad,
There's always a way to recycle today.

The Earth will be saved, thanks to you
If you make the effort and think before you do.

Amy Craig-Wood (12)
Prior's Field School, Godalming

It Used To Be

The world used to be green
But now it's grey
And murky from pollution.

Wildlife used to thrive
But now it seems sad
And empty with nothing.

This world used to be clean
But now it seems
Dirty with no colour.

We need to plant trees.
We need to save the animals.
We need to clean up now.
We will make a difference.

Ellen Ferguson (12)
Prior's Field School, Godalming

What Am I?

I am black, but my friends are red,
I am rank and at the same time rotting.

I have been pulled ad thrown around nearly every week,
Things are always around me but I still feel alone.

I have always got stuff in me, I am never clean
And I caused more pollution when I was born.

What am I?

A: Black recycling bin.

Tamara Chiltern-Hunt (12)
Prior's Field School, Godalming

Warfare - Pointless

W eapons being used to kill normal people day by day.
A wful war started for no reason.
R easoning seems out of reach.
F ires started to burn towns.
A nybody know why this war started?
R eturning things to the way they were seems impossible.
E dible food running out.

Stuart Boulton (15)
Rowdeford Special School, Devizes

The Animal Kingdom

The world is in a nightmare, the end is coming, all *life* will be gone
Only we can save our blue and green world from the darkness
Be brave as a tiger, have the wings of a bird, still as a gecko
All the animal kingdom needs help to be safe from evil
All the animal kingdom is falling and the end of *life* is coming
Is a second chance OK?

Matthew Goodyear (15)
Rowdeford Special School, Devizes

Endangered

E nraged environmentalists.
N ew problems.
D ead species due to poaching.
A fter what we have done to the planet, we need to turn the tide (literally!)
N o matter how bad it looks, we can still reverse the damage.
G ood things come to those who wait.
E very time we try to make things better, we make it worse (by accident).
R aving on about global warming and how bad it is.
E nding this bad time will be very hard.
D ark times lie ahead.

Julian Emery (15)
Rowdeford Special School, Devizes

If We Could Stop

If we could stop war
If we could stop extinction
If we could stop pollution
If we could stop racism
If we could stop people being homeless
If we could stop animals dying out
If we could stop dying rainforests
If we could stop poverty
If we could stop climate change
The world would be a better place.

Jake Sidwell (15)
Rowdeford Special School, Devizes

Pollution

L ying upon the street
I t really is a mess
T ime to do something
T owns and cities alike
E veryone join in
R eturn our streets to sanity

F ound as dangerous
A mateurs work there
C lever ones
T he ones to see an end come
O n these factories
R ebels are the ones
I nventing new ways
E co comes in
S aving the day.

Joshua Gasan (12)
St Peter's RC High School, Gloucester

Green

Green, green, green what a wonderful colour
Green, green, green it could not be duller
Although a wonderful colour, the black has taken over
And we can't run for safe cover.

Thanks to us the world is melting
While we're still going the world is tilting
Standby's no good, turn the lights off
The world is being wiped with a cloth.

William Thomas (12)
St Peter's RC High School, Gloucester

Recycle Humans

The beginning of the endless end,
Humans have started,
The green nature is winning,
But not as it wanted.

The human race is gaining,
Gaining knowledge to survive,
But will this knowledge just help to survive,
Or starve the Earth with no guilt in the eye?

The middle of the end,
The wars have started,
The power people gain,
Isn't just for justice.

The end is closing,
Closing in with poverty and pollution,
Closing in with mindless thoughts,
Which gives Earth not much of a choice.

The end has happened,
Happening again and destroying,
Destroying the life on Earth,
Which takes the human race back to nature.

But how can we stop
The cycle of human race,
Which will make
The Earth a better place?

Nick Kowal (12)
St Peter's RC High School, Gloucester

Making The World A Better Place

We should make the world a better place,
Do something every day.
It doesn't matter what we look like,
Or where we want to play.

We should recycle all our rubbish,
To keep things nice and green.
Come on, let's all do this,
We'll do it as a team.

Global warming is a problem
We really need to solve.
We need to work together,
Get everyone involved.

If we do these little things,
It will make a difference.
The world will be a better place,
For all of its existence.

Ellie Lister (12)
St Peter's RC High School, Gloucester

Third World

A pinch of perfection or a gallon of guilt?
A mass of money or no homes to be built?
A cupful of community or a palm of poverty?
A pan of power or the young scavenging?
A respected race or restless racism?
A long-lived life or no heart rhythm?
A place to go or no one to go to?
A close family always together
Or a world that will never live forever . . . never ever!

Sinéad Dangerfield (12)
St Peter's RC High School, Gloucester

A Better Place Without War

Imagine the world
With no war,
Imagine peace
And no one scared.

Imagine if everyone
Had the same rights,
Imagine if nobody
Was getting killed.

Imagine if everyone
Had a home,
If no one's house
Was getting destroyed.

Why do we go to war?
What, do we want more?

Jem Winter (12)
St Peter's RC High School, Gloucester

Earth

The Earth is ours to enjoy
For every little girl and boy.
But we must always be aware
That all its beauty we must share
With all the children yet to come,
Who want to laugh and play and run
Around the trees and in the fields.

So we must keep our planet free
From messy trash and debris,
With air that's clean and fresh and clear
For all to breathe from year to year.
We must never ever abuse
Our sweet Earth that's ours to use.

Josh Mustoe-Linnane (12)
St Peter's RC High School, Gloucester

Everything Is Going

My home is going, family gone.
My food is gone, will I go?
The trees are falling, men are coming.
Where is the rain? This is not rain; it burns your skin, makes you cry.
The noises are getting closer, what are they?
Falling, crashing, the trees are going.
The men have come with machines, pushing, pulling the trees down.
They are here, I am going.
I am gone.

William Murphy (12)
St Peter's RC High School, Gloucester

Call From A Voice

Charity
'To give
Your choice,'
Came from a little voice

Racism
'Colour offence
Sometimes not our choice,'
Came a call from a little voice

Homeless,
What to do?
A small voice called,
'It's up to you!'

Peace
Live in harmony
'Is that wrong?'
Came out of my voice.

Nasty about difference
That's not OK
We're all people anyway.

Cameron Morgan (12)
St Peter's RC High School, Gloucester

Death To A Planet

The smoke rising from the towers of despair,
My lungs are black from dust and gas.
The earthquakes are my anger,
The birds are my peace.
The cars and lorries roaring along the coat of the Earth,
The forests are in terror.
My creatures are going towards the mist of extinction,
The seas are black like the smoke of war.
Depression, depression is all I can think of,
Why not save me?
The materials they use for glass and plastic,
Why not save the bottle, the shoe?
The never-ending rubbish is like the rows of traffic,
The acid rain drenching away my virgin forests.
Why?

Joseph Jennings (12)
St Peter's RC High School, Gloucester

Homelessness!

H omelessness,
O ld lady sitting in the street,
M addy is her name,
E very day and every night is the same - alone,
L eft alone she was, every day, every night,
E ach bin she looks through for a scrap to eat,
S he has no family, 'they all hate me',
S ix bags of belongings is all she saved,
N o one loves her, needs her, cares for her,
E ach night she cries thinking about her future,
S treet pavement is her bed, old blanket for warmth,
'S end someone to look and care for me.'

Katy Coughlan (12)
St Peter's RC High School, Gloucester

The Homeless!

Alone again,
No one to hold tight,
All because of that little fight,
No one to blame.

My husband's gone,
I think because of that bomb,
He went off to war
And left me homeless and poor.

My life was on the mend
Until it turned that bend,
I'm scavenging for food
And I'm never in a happy mood.

Still no one to blame,
As I still lie here cold and lame.
Why me? I feel so ashamed,
I beg you to come home, I pray.

Ollie Edwards (12)
St Peter's RC High School, Gloucester

Litter

L eaving garbage everywhere
I rony for the planet
T errible things happening right in front of our eyes
T rash scattered all over the planet
E arth and everything on it dying
R otting away everything that ever existed.

Theo Neuschwander (12)
St Peter's RC High School, Gloucester

Milk And Ash

Sweat drops onto bone-dry ground
Slashing and screams are the only sound
Pure red wine in a golden cup
And heavy iron being lifted up
Juicy grapes eaten in front of children's eyes
While others will never see bright blue skies
Bitter chocolate bodies in a pile
Other piles around it that go on for miles and miles
Dim-eyed crows fly overhead
Ready to feast on the dead

Velvet, silk and marble floors
Six servants opening heavy oak doors
Balconies with a view like the sun
Humongous rooms only for one
China plates with cups of tea
Being sipped next to the bright blue sea
Elegance, poise, room to dance
Cloudless skies perfect for romance
Selfish, powerful, very wealthy
Something slaves will never be.

Lucy Keal (12)
St Peter's RC High School, Gloucester

Injustice

I n a cold cell, alone in the dark,
N ever to be free again,
J unk for food,
U ndervalued and utterly useless,
S lammed by the law, all against me,
T ormented by the culprit he stalks me day by day,
I naccurately portrayed,
C ontinuous torture for one mistake,
E nough is enough!

Henry Cole (13)
Sandringham School, St Albans

Being Green

On the news there's only doom
Credit crunch, financial gloom.

But the silver lining of this state
Is the greenness forced upon our plate.

No longer can we waste and spend
Those days of excess must now end.

Cut down on baths or have a shower
Recycle waste, turn off the power.

iPods, laptops, mobiles too
Do we need them all day through?

Donate to charity that old thing
It might be someone else's bling!

Walk or cycle, leave the car
We'll all be better off by far!

Buy food in season, local veg
Or grow your own, straight from the hedge.

The greenest person that I know
Has been like this since long ago.

Having lived through war years frugally
My granny's green automatically!

James Riding (12)
Sandringham School, St Albans

It's Our Choice

This world is wrong, this world is in doubt,
We need to save the planet before time runs out.
The Earth is getting hotter, getting burnt by the sun
And no one cares that the worst is still to come.
Animals are dying, they need our protection,
But to help our world, we need some connection!

Lydia Spooner (13)
Sandringham School, St Albans

My Voice

The world is not just black and white,
Personality will always shine bright.
Be true to yourself endlessly,
Think of the world positively.

One man cannot stand alone,
Everybody has a tone.
The world can be a better place,
Don't judge people on size, gender or race.

Because we're all the same in different ways,
Discrimination is just a phase.
Make a dream and see it through,
Treat people how people treat you.

So do something good today,
Save the world in every way.

Kerry Dyer (12)
Tewkesbury School, Tewkesbury

Our World

Flowing rivers of the clearest blue
Fresh grass coating the ground
Trees standing tall and strong
Colourful flowers growing all around
Hills towering on the horizon
White wispy clouds floating by
People and animals all happy
The sun shining in the sky

Brown, dirty, clogged up rivers
Sooty, smoky, dusty air
The countryside covered in litter
People causing it without a care
Plants are dying and the colour's gone
Gloomy, dull faces is all you can see
Factories billowing black smoke
What would you like our world to be?

Kate Brookes (12)
Tewkesbury School, Tewkesbury

Anilife

A hit cat
A frightened bat
A hurt dog
A squished frog
A noisy car
A night at the bar
The laughter rings
A disregarding driver
A life depriver
Kill an animal
Take a life
Do they care?

Lesley McDowall (13)
Tewkesbury School, Tewkesbury

Always Time For A Change

Ice cubes melting
Drifting into the heated sea
Swirling snowstorms
Transform into fluttering tears
Fossil fuel sources run dry
Pencil-lined smoke
Blown out of giant cigars
Slowly squeezing out
Spluttering breaths, from the wheezy planet.

Ebony clouds bring acid rain
Chipping away at solemn statues
Crystal-blue oceans
Turn speckled brown with waste and oil
The ripped ozone layer begins to tire
Rainforests falling, gasping for air
Endangered animals asking for help
The Earth, our Earth
Care for it, as it cares for us
Now is our time to change.

Hannah Ballard (12)
Tewkesbury School, Tewkesbury

I Am The Earth

I am the Earth, listen to me
It's hard to believe that once I was free
It was peaceful, till you came along
You evolved and became too strong
All of the life that I had once before
Is deteriorating fast and will soon be no more
Your cars and your gas and your electricity
You reign supreme and it's destroying me
I let you in to obtain my trust
Kill your own kind, if you must
I am the Earth, listen to me
Leave me alone, just let me be.

Lauren Pickford (12)
Tewkesbury School, Tewkesbury

Footsteps Of The Ape

As I look through the bars at the ever-changing world,
It's hot in the day and then ice-cold, as I lie curled.
Looking up at night at the silent and glimmering stars, such peace.
I long to be safe.

Safe from people sneering and shouting,
Looking at me as if I will rage.
Scared to move, tired of noises,
And no space to move in my cage.

Kind faces and kind eyes peering at me,
And when I wake I feel warmth, I'm free,
Free to live the life of a monkey,
With friends, keepers and safe to be me.

Holly Squires (12)
The Arts Educational School, London

Homeless

Bangs, clangs and men's shouts,
Twigs and leaves flying through the air,
Clouds of dust,
The old oak tree is being cut down.

All the neighbours complained,
My parents hated it,
Now a homeless fox runs up to me,
He can't find his family.

A leaflet through the door, a few weeks later,
Small black boy on the front,
He's in the midst of rubble,
His 'once was' home.

What's that in the distance?
Big grey tanks,
Mummy's gone now,
What shall he do?

Bang, bang . . .
Brrrrr . . .
Yells and laughs,
Screams and insults.

It's all over,
Clouds of dust,
They were here for two days,
He's alone.

I understand now,
How it must feel,
Alone and afraid,
No family, no home.

Marie Claire De Voil (11)
The Arts Educational School, London

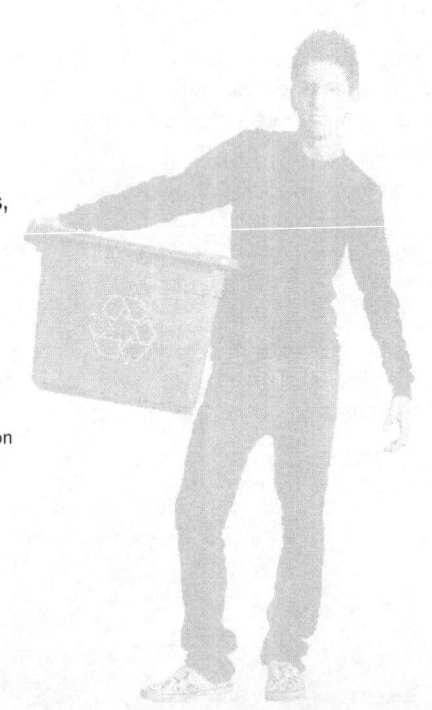

Plastic Bottles
(To be read to the tune of 'Baggy Trousers' by Madness)

Plastic bottles and tin cans,
Unused paper, rubber bands.
Rotting food and glass as well,
Fish that really makes it smell.

Orange peel and magazines,
Old ripped clothes and tangerines.
Paper cuttings, bottle caps,
Broken this and broken that.

Do we really know,
What happens when we let it go?
We think it's normal,
But it's not at all.
Do we really know,
What happens when we let it go?
We think it's normal,
But it's not at all.

Plastic bottles,
Plastic bottles,
Plastic bottles,
Recycle.

Colbert Newsome (13)
The Arts Educational School, London

Cut Out The Cars!

We drive our cars every day,
Why not try our bikes,
Not throw them away.
Or try the bus it's not that bad
And don't forget about the legs we have,
They weren't made to sit around all day,
They should be out walking around.
Okay!
Our world is becoming a cloud of smoke,
We should 'cut out the cars' before we *choke!*

Ella Stephens (11)
The Arts Educational School, London

Bang! Bash! Boom!

Bang! Bash! Boom!
Then silence.
The whole world stops and stares.
Bang! Bash! Boom!
Then quietness.
A chorus heard everywhere.
Bang! Bash! Boom!
Then stillness.
Will it never end?
Bang! Bash! Boom!
Then sadness.
I have lost my only friend.
Bang! Bash! Boom!
I cry.
Bullets fly everywhere.
Bang! Bash! Boom!
Then pain
And everything goes dark.
I feel myself falling.
I want to run
But I can't.
Bang! Bash! Boom!
Then nothing.
The noise has stopped at last.

Antonia Blakeman (13)
The Arts Educational School, London

It's Hard (A Homeless Poem)

It's hard to raise your head, when your pillow is made from stone,
It's hard to get a job when you're all alone,
It's hard to eat your food when you have none
And it's hard to find peace when all the peace is gone.

Georgia M Elvin (11)
The Arts Educational School, London

The Sound Of War

I hear the sound of war,
The guns, the bombs, they roar,
I hear this frightening sound,
Dead bodies all around.

People running, people scared,
Death coming for them is what they shared,
The sound of war's a frightening sound,
They see dead bodies all around.

Where is everybody now?
They're all lying on the ground,
Never to be seen again,
Dead. Gone. Forever.

Eve Burns (13)
The Arts Educational School, London

A Greener World

Oh the litter, we need to get rid,
Turn the world green and hybrid,
Make the world greater, whatever kind of race,
To make the world a better place
We've got to get rid of this pollution.

Surely there's a greener solution,
C'mon now, don't waste that paper,
Recycle it, use it later.

Don't waste the water, turn off the taps,
Think about the polar ice caps,
What about all this oil and war?
And all this killing for more and more,
So make the world greener, get on your bike
Or your grandkids will be saying,
'What did a polar bear look like?

Freddie Mark Anthony (13)
The Arts Educational School, London

Walking Around The World

As I walk around the world,
From top to bottom, round and round.
What has happened?
The rainforests are on fire, burning my feet.
Pollution in the air, stopping me breathe.
Poverty destroying people, no money, no life.
Litter flying, flapping, trapping, hurting
And what can we do?

Guns, knives, bombs and war, what's it for?
My ears are pierced by the harsh words of a racist voice.
We are blinded by our own lives but now I see,
Some people don't have a home like me.
There's two words I keep hearing, everywhere I go . . .
Climate change
And what can we do?

Protect the rainforests, my feet stop burning
Stop polluting, I can breathe again.
Help people, give to charity, they have their lives back.
Put your litter in a bin, stop hurting.
Stop all the wars, what are they for?

Let's bring us together, we'll find answers for our futures.
All nations, from north, south, east, west,
Black or white and all the rest.

Emilia Campanale (13)
The Arts Educational School, London

Think

While you are lying in your bed,
A poor poverty-suffering person is lying dead.

While you are wearing your clothes,
Eating your food, sitting in your house.

'They' are crouching in their shack,
Wearing rags and eating about enough for a mouse.

So next time you don't finish your vegetables
Or moan about what you wanted
But didn't get for Christmas, think . . .

Mei Borg-Cardona (12)
The Arts Educational School, London

Poverty And Being Homeless

I have no home, I sleep in a den.
People hold their noses when they go past me.
I scavenge for food in supermarket bins
And I have no friends or family.
My mum died when I was four
But we didn't have a phone to call anyone.
I hold a cup but I only get pennies
So I can only buy one sweet.
I need help because I have a cracked tooth
It aches and aches night and day
But I can't smile properly.
I never smile anyway 'cause there's nothing to smile at.
I need help.

Whitney Svosve (11)
The Arts Educational School, London

But Together We Cry

Don't you think it's time to calm down?
Wars have been declared, now it's a fight,
For power, money and territory, yeah that's right.
We're killing each other over race, pride and respect,
Doesn't this make a big effect?
Children in Africa starving, doesn't this make you sad?
When everything we do is just so we make ourselves glad.
Gangs destroying this world with everyday killings.
Drinking and smoking at the age of thirteen
And every side corner of a street
You see a homeless person's cold, dirty feet.
Slowly polluting the world,
With wars, poverty, racism and fear,
We're destroying the atmosphere
But together we cry.

Grace D'arcy Craig (13)
The Arts Educational School, London

Spinning Around

The world is spinning round and round,
But we don't know the changes it makes.
Sometimes you can feel helpless, angry and sad.
You can also feel scared.
Bang! Bang! Down goes a man,
A knife is pulled out. I turn to my right, scream,
Turn to my left, more screams.
Everyone around me is shocked. 'It wasn't me, I promise!'
I take one step forward
And there that word goes again and again; *racism.*
Everyone is the same, loved for who they are.
People don't need to be treated differently
Because of their skin colour or the background they belong to.
It's time to start again, make a fresh start
And then the world will be a better place.

Yasemin Alkan (13)
The Arts Educational School, London

Off

Turn off the tap when you brush your teeth,
Turn off the lights as you leave the room.
Turn off the kettle once you've made your coffee,
Turn off the oven when you have made your tea.

Turn off the computer once you've done your work,
Turn off the telly if you hate the show.
Turn off the radio when it's time to go,
Turn on your brains for it's a brand new day.

Arthur Williams (13)
The Arts Educational School, London

A Sleepless Night

Endless nights of hunger and cold,
Feel the chill in the night air.
Food is scarce and covered in mould,
Damp and messy is your hair.

No one really cares for you,
They leave you outside alone.
Scared and tired, thirsty too,
Soaked and cold, down to the bone.

Shivering frantically, hugging your knees,
You're cold and wet, there's no one there.
Crying softly, you hide from the sharp breeze,
Ragged clothes, your arms bare.

Dripping and dirty is your face,
You push your hair out of your eyes.
All you can feel is the lonely space,
You hope someone hears your helpless cries.

Susannah Pike (12)
The Arts Educational School, London

Smile With The Environment

Light wind brushes the thin green grass
As the sun smiles at everyone.
The happiness gets spread like a good disease
And makes the whole world think, smile, believe.

There should be no hesitation to make the world a better place.
Helping the environment is easiest
When you're tackling it with a smile.

Conor Tychowski (11)
The Buckingham School, Buckingham

No War

W hy do we have war to show which country is best?
A nnoyed to think people are so evil
   trying to blow our country and start war.
R ed is the colour of blood,
   no, red should be the colour of roses.

We should stop war now!

Aidan Deeney (11)
The Buckingham School, Buckingham

Wars Stop Now!

Where does war get you?
Nowhere, nowhere.
We need peace not wars.
Peace is what we need.
What are you doing to our planet?
Killing it, polluting it,
So stop war!

Jasmine Swain (12)
The Buckingham School, Buckingham

Pollution Is Everywhere

Pollution, pollution is in the air.
Pollution, pollution is everywhere.
We are running out of time,
We have nowhere to climb
To get away from the horrible mess.
Someone will have to stand up
And ... *confess!*

Megan Horsler (11)
The Buckingham School, Buckingham

Stop!

As I lay on my bed I hear gunshots and people screaming
I wonder why there are people screaming and gunshots
Help the world we live in.
Stop, put down your guns and stop what you're doing.
As the wars carry on I don't see the point
Why do people keep dying for other people's mistakes.

Paul Booth (11)
The Buckingham School, Buckingham

Save Us!

Recycling is always new,
It's just one way that you can help too.

Bike to school, it's good for you,
Or even walk a mile or two.

Money isn't everything,
Some people don't even have it,
So why don't you? I'll give you a clue,
Donate a penny or a few.

Help yourself and the world as well,
Don't hesitate to do so.
It's always good to try something new
So go out there and do it!

Katie Wood (11)
The Buckingham School, Buckingham

Global Warming

G lobal warming is bad.
L osing our Earth's animals to extinction.
O zone layer is melting.
B e environmentally friendly.
A nnoyed at people who litter.
L ittering will ruin the future.

W hy litter?
A re you littering now?
R ecycle cans and get money.
M ake the world a better place.
I magine what you could achieve.
N o one has the right to spoil the Earth.
G lad products tell you to put waste in bins.

Daniel Rainsbury (11)
The Buckingham School, Buckingham

Litter

L ots of packaging takes a long time to rot so recycle it!
I magine all the litter we are producing,
where are we going to put it?
T hink what will happen when we don't have any space
to put all the rubbish
T he Earth won't be able to cope.
E veryone can help by . . .
R ecycling to make the world a cleaner, happier place.

Holly Tucker (11)
The Buckingham School, Buckingham

Save The World

If you can't stop choking
Of course stop smoking
It's better if you recycle
And ride on a bicycle
Don't throw rubbish on the ground
It's bad for the world all around
Don't think you won't be caught
If you are angry and sad
Tell people don't be so bad
If you don't want to live in a dump
Give it a try - recycle
You can help the world a lot.

Connor Luke Bennett (11)
The Buckingham School, Buckingham

Respect Everything

We all do something wrong,
There is a way we can fix it,
This is all about our world,
How we can change it.

There is graffiti on the walls,
Also rubbish filling,
We are being bad to the animals
So let's stop now!

Soon we will have no countryside left,
So we will have no animals.
No animals means no meat,
So we need to treat everything with respect.

So treat everything with respect,
We will have a better place.
Start now or it could be too late,
So do treat everything with respect.

Simon George (11)
The Buckingham School, Buckingham

The Horrible Truth

The world is dying
And you are to blame
I feel like crying
You should feel the same
The trees, the plants and animals are about to disappear
And you don't try to stop this mess
That is what I fear
So do it now, you must confess
There is no time to wait
So bike to school, don't use the car
Or find another way
And doing this will go so far
Listen to what I say
So get together and make the world a better place
Because you must help save our race.

Harry Akerman (11)
The Buckingham School, Buckingham

Our World And Other's

If you like to litter,
You are just purely bitter,
If you can find a bin,
Pick it up and stick it in.
Think how people feel,
You might want to think,
That might give you a tip,
This is how people feel,
Sad, worried, upset and annoyed,
They feel like this because it's also their environment,
If you never walk,
You don't need to talk,
Because the only word I can say is *lazy*.
Think about the world,
Also the ozone layer,
If you live near a shop don't be lazy,
Take a nice long or short walk.

Georgie Gibbard-Bray (11)
The Buckingham School, Buckingham

Pollution

As the climate boils above
we fail to see what we have begun.

As our grandchildren are left with this mess
They may not find the solution to success.

But if we act on this problem instead of later
Our grandchildrens future will be much greater.

While if we don't act on this dilemma
The whole world may be lost forever.

Stephen Ettery (13)
The Buckingham School, Buckingham

Leads To Change

Changes occur every day.
Soon children won't be able to go out and play.
One little piece of junk left on a beach
Or factories pumping out a bit of waste.
This bit of waste will lead to more.

Pollution leads to bad changes.
Pollution leads to climate change.
Climate change kills off animals
So soon there will be no animal race.

You can't rely on one person to change this
So let's work together and stop it today.
If you dispose of that little bit of junk
You will be stopping all kinds of bad change
Which helps to make the world a better place.

Stuart Ironmonger (13)
The Buckingham School, Buckingham

… YoungWriters

We're Losing Them!

Wet, cold, sunny and dry
I do let out a sigh,
As I see homeless dogs trying to fight, but why?
Why don't we let them in,
Into our heart, where they will win?
Why do we let them die cold?
They should be in the heat,
Standing out *bold*.

Homeless dogs, we will not see
We are killing them, don't you see?
They will be extinct,
They will be gone,
Gone from our hearts,
As fast as go-karts.

I just want a pet,
A pet I can keep,
A pet for a day,
A pet for a life.

So here it comes,
Extinction is here,
We should be in fear
Because now it's here
So stop and think
So your heart sinks
Into the dangers of becoming extinct!

Kayley Roberts (14)
The Buckingham School, Buckingham

Too Many Angels In The Sky

There are too many angels in the sky
Who sent them up there?
Who let them die?
They were only little, they were only small,
Who let them leave?
Who let them fall?

We're all responsible, you and I,
We're the reason
There's too many angels in the sky.

Please help to end these wars,
Let's look after people and keep them warm,
Keep them healthy, strong and living!
Then maybe if we all help
There won't be as many angels in the sky,
Maybe they'll survive.

We're all responsible, you and I,
We're the reason
There's too many angels in the sky.

Megan Thompson (13)
The Buckingham School, Buckingham

Open Your Eyes!

What did we do to this world so fine?
Choking a planet so wonderful, so divine.

Think to yourself as you read this rhyme,
What are we doing at this current time?
Crippling this world with a deadly fume,
Before we know it, it will be over soon.

What did we do to this world so fine?
Choking a planet so wonderful, so divine.

Paper, glass and cans, recycle the lot,
If we don't do it soon we may as well be shot,
The world will not stand for our terrible waste,
We carry on like this and we will be out with haste.

What did we do to this world so fine?
Choking a planet so wonderful, so divine.

In our wars with guns and blood,
Cold bodies hit the floor with a huge thud,
Families destroyed with the pull of a trigger,
The dead man list is getting bigger and bigger.

What did we do to this world so fine?
Choking a planet so wonderful, so divine.

In this rhyme, I hope you now see,
The end of the world may rely on you and me,
So make a change to the world today
And let our grandchildren dance and play.

Open your eyes!

Marcus Prodanovic (13)
The Buckingham School, Buckingham

The Solution Is A Smile

I turned around a corner,
To see what's hiding there,
Poverty, pollution, suffering,
More than I could bear.

Children screaming, crying,
Not sure what to do or say,
Will the world ever go back
To how it was yesterday?

The traffic, cars,
Pollution, hunger and money,
Some cry or think it a joke,
But this problem is not funny.

Is this all true, is it fake?
These feelings that we feel,
To help one another,
To make it all really real.

To next time you go out walking,
Just think for a while,
When you see a sad person,
Give them a small smile.

Rhiannon Taylor (13)
The Buckingham School, Buckingham

A Brighter Future

Our planet is slowly dying.
It's time to start trying.
Let's stop pollution and littering too
And make the world a better place for you.
Let's take responsibility now
And make our future brighter.

It's easy to do your part,
So come on, let's make a start.
Turn the television off at the plug,
When cold, use blankets to keep you snug.
It's simple really, use less electricity
And make our future brighter.

So that's pollution dealt with, phew!
To stop littering's simple too.
Just wait for the next bin around,
Instead of dropping it on the ground.
You could even start to recycle
And make our future brighter.

Emma Brazier (14)
The Buckingham School, Buckingham

Your World, Our World

Everyone living their lives, they don't care,
Just acting so normal, still unaware,
Do they know what they are doing to their world, our world?
Everything they read; global warming, going green,
They don't know what all this means,
So they just live their own lives!

The Earth is calling out,
Who knows what it's all about?
We are killing our home,
The Earth feels so alone.
And it's calling out for our help!

You want to help the world?
Then don't just sit back,
People who want to make a difference, that's what we lack,
Just pick up some litter,
Please don't be bitter
And help your world, our world, today!

Bryony Foote (13)
The Buckingham School, Buckingham

That's All Folks

Thanks Dad
For everything you've done
You've left me to clear up the mess
Now that you've had your fun.

Others look down upon us
Our youth is getting worse
But really who's the villain
That caused the greenhouse curse.

I've gone out of my way
To help someone other than myself
You've doomed a future generation
And left me sitting on the shelf.

So maybe think again
Not of how we're strange
But how we're saving the world
By stopping climate change.

That's all folks!

Robert Lukey (13)
The Buckingham School, Buckingham

What Is Going To Happen If . . .

Throw away bottles, papers and cans,
Or pollute the Earth, the seas and the land,
Kill everything from blue to green
And every living thing you've ever seen.

Animals and humans will die pretty soon,
From babies to grannies, from snakes, to baboons,
But if we recycle maybe they won't,
But help us please, we'll die if you don't!

This day, today could be our last,
To take a breath, to puff, to gasp,
So if we don't recycle our bottles and paper,
You'll be sorry later.

If you want to live, please recycle!

Abigail Young (13)
The Buckingham School, Buckingham

Our Linking World

It started off as names,
It then went into frames
And now it's turning into a punch,
Whenever they want my money for lunch.

I try to tell my form tutor,
But how do I explain to her,
That anything I do or anything I say,
Can't keep their fists away.

Is it because of my coloured race,
That I am getting this hurtful face.
But inside me I have a heavy frown,
How can I turn it upside down?

This is how our wars are started,
Where different coloured people are parted.
That's how we can all turn this frown
Into a smile upside down!

Jade Heritage (13)
The Buckingham School, Buckingham

Would You Pull The Trigger?

Would you pull the trigger,
On a lion or a big cat
For the sake of a fur coat
Or a fluffy, woolly hat?

The Yangtze pink river dolphin
Has just become extinct
Entangled in the nets
We use to catch the fish we eat.

Many of the great apes
Are dying out too
Their babies are taken
To be a pet for you.

The elephants and rhinos
Are becoming very rare
Because they are shot
For the ivory they bare.

Even the frogs
Are disappearing too
We pollute their ponds
I care about them, do you?

Amber Wieland (13)
The Buckingham School, Buckingham

Help The World

Help the environment,
Help the environment,
By helping the environment,
You help the world!

Ageism, racism, the victim's pain,
Ageism, racism, pain is gained,
Ageism, racism, black, white or blue,
Ageism, racism, we're all like you!

The ice caps are melting, what does this mean?
The ice caps are melting, we need to turn green,
Cut down pollution, recycle as well,
The ice caps are melting, no time to dwell.

Extinction, extinction, you should feel remorse,
T-rex, the dodo, the dawn horse,
Extinction, extinction, listen to me,
Extinction, extinction, cut down hunting, that's the key.

The future, the future, we're ruining it,
The future, the future, bit by bit,
The future, the future, it's help we need,
The future, the future, let's make it better!

The world, the world, we *can* make it better,
The world, the world, if we work together,
The world, the world, let's turn green,
The world, the world, people are in need!

Help the environment,
Help the environment,
By helping the environment,
You help the world!

Hayley Siklodi (14)
The Buckingham School, Buckingham

Get Earth On The Mend

Tomorrow never comes
But soon it will end,
We need to make a difference,
Get Earth on the mend.

When we are old and wrinkly
Close to leaving this world behind,
We will look back and punish ourselves
For not being too kind.

Dinosaurs and dodos,
Tasmanian wolves too,
All of these no longer around
And there is nothing we can do.

Boiling hot weather,
Ice is melting fast,
Do we have a future
Or just a scorching past?

We might not be aware
Or it might be crystal clear,
That many children across the world
Are living in danger and fear.

You may not be affected
By this very serious case,
But the thing that you should really know,
We are slowly killing the human race.

Tomorrow never comes
But soon it will end,
We need to make a difference,
Get Earth on the mend.

Lucy Piosek (13)
The Buckingham School, Buckingham

It's In Our Hands

I shan't force you to listen,
We all hear it each day,
But perhaps just stop and think . . .
Take in what they say.

We may not be affected,
Or even our daughters or sons,
But it's our great-great-great grandchildren
Who suffer what's to come.

In a world that's so hot,
All animals have died out,
Where water is scarce,
The whole world in a drought.

And who will they blame?
Not Mother Nature but us.
Why didn't we stop it,
When we had the chance?

This is not the only option
It could be prevented.
If the safety of Earth,
Our generation cemented.

So no pressure or anything,
It's our elders who did this.
So come on,
What are we waiting for?
Let's be the ones to fix it!

I shan't force you to listen,
But listen you might
And let your great-great-great grandchildren
Sleep sound one more night.

Gaia Ward (13)
The Buckingham School, Buckingham

Stop Knife Crime

K ill knife crime,
N ever carry a knife,
I n prison - no one likes it,
F ighting - don't get involved,
E njoy life.

C rime is not the way to entertain yourself,
R unning away - don't make people do it,
I nvolve everyone in fun and games,
M ove away from people with knives,
E ncourage people to stop carrying knives.

Just stop it!

Jack Balch (11)
The Hazeley School, Milton Keynes

Why Do People Do These Things?

Litter, litter everywhere
Litter, litter over there
Being homeless is not fun
Pollution is what everyone has done
Animals becoming extinct
Why do people do these things?
Rainforests being cut down
Climate change is all around
Racism must be stopped
Poverty can become a lot
Recycling is what can help
But not enough to save our world
All we need is everyone's help
And stop our pollution.

Sophie Robertson (12)
The Hazeley School, Milton Keynes

Global Warming

Soon the water will dry out
And there will be a drought
The solution?
Stop pollution!

Don't leave litter
It is really bitter
Global warming
Time for a warning!

Liam Coleman (11)
The Hazeley School, Milton Keynes

Street Walk

Walking down a windy street
Empty drink cans rolling down the gutter
A carrier bag wraps around my feet
I try to talk but I stutter.

A fox runs in front of me
I notice a rope around his leg
Should I help it or leave it be?
I walk past a tatty shop,
Its window splattered with eggs.

Rubbish bags lying in the road
No one to be seen day or night
The few dustcarts barely get loaded
Then I get a really big fright.

Lucy Abraham (11)
The Hazeley School, Milton Keynes

The Big Green Recycling Machine

Being good means being green.
Not being mean, just do something green.
Like recycling plastic, glass and metal.
Gives enough electricity to put on a kettle.
Recycling paper will be really good.
It will save the trees in the neighbourhood.

Amy Hewitson (11)
The Hazeley School, Milton Keynes

Hope For The Future?

There she lies at the end of the street
No home, no food, no love.
Here come the binmen loading the bin sacks
But where are the pink bags?

Another day at school, or another day at war?
Black versus white, white versus black.
Poverty and AIDS all in one,
What could be worse?

Cars, gas, chimneys and well you name it,
It's basically all the things changing the sky colour.
More paper, less trees, more saws, less oxygen,
Result - no nature or life!

Charlotte Straker (11)
The Hazeley School, Milton Keynes

Girl

Look at her, she was there on Monday
And now she is here again on Sunday.
Look at her clothes, they're no more than rags.
She has all of her belongings in carrier bags.
When I look at her face she looks so empty and sad.
She makes me feel so terribly bad.
She shivers with fear when anyone comes near.
She is a lost soul with no home and no goal.

Georgia Barnes (11)
The Hazeley School, Milton Keynes

Smoking

Smoking everywhere,
Smoking all the time,
What I would call
A horrible crime.

People buying them,
People selling them,
If you don't know what is in it,
You should bin it.

Smelling it everywhere,
Seeing it everywhere,
Watching people's heart rates go down
Because people are smoking their life slows down.

George Boland (12)
The Hazeley School, Milton Keynes

What Could Happen?

E very time we drive cars it causes pollution
N ever time to rewind the clock
   when something bad happens to the world
V ariety of people want to do something about it, so why don't you?
I n every country something bad happens to the world,
   because of what they do.
R emember we are doing the damage.
O ur environment could be better than we make it.
N othing will happen, only if we do something now.
M oment by moment the world is dying.
E veryone should think about what they are doing for the future.
N early every time we let out smoke it will affect the world.
T reat the world a lot better.

Dana Davey (11)
The Hazeley School, Milton Keynes

A Better Place

The world is changing
The time is near
For us to come and interfere

Save the forests
Stop the waste
So we can save our time and place

Change the climate
Help the children
Who have been sleeping rough and bitter

I've done my bit
Now time for yours
To help and change the world.

Gail Dechochai (11)
The Hazeley School, Milton Keynes

Rubbish

Rubbish, rubbish everywhere,
Watch the people stop and stare,
At the humungous pile,
And you have to admit,
It's very vile.
Rubbish, rubbish everywhere,
Does anyone care?

Emma Hoare (11)
The Hazeley School, Milton Keynes

Littering

Every day people drop their rubbish on the ground,
No one cares about the fact the planet's going down.

We're always being told to pick things up,
To stop throwing things, to pick up all our muck.

You hear things on the news, about the planet falling apart,
If you start acting now you'll become a real superstar!

It's destroying the wildlife, it's not very fair,
Many people in this world don't really care.

Emily Brown (11)
The Hazeley School, Milton Keynes

About Our Environment

The environment is very important to the future of our planet Earth.
We must try to save it for all its worth.

Forests are being killed because we use too many trees.
We must not waste paper but use it carefully please.

We waste lots of light by leaving them on.
Turn them off and they will last very long.

Try and recycle and picture the world in your hands.

Rebekah Harris (11)
The Hazeley School, Milton Keynes

In The Wind

In the wind, a little girl plays,
Thinking of the world changing in all different ways,
Looking at the clouds, looking down low,
She stops running fast and starts walking slow.
In the wind, a little boy gasps,
Falling in shock on the crisp-dry grass,
The young boy opens his patio gate,
He and the girl wonder,
'Can the world be saved . . . or is it too late?'
These children's world is being destroyed,
Can we help them or will it be ignored?

Taylor Gordon (11)
The Hazeley School, Milton Keynes

The Environment Before And After

Before

I can see broken trees,
Lots of rubbish and lots of dead flowers,
I can smell lots of rotten food,
Lots of dirt and dead animals,
I can hear nothing at all
Even when it is sunny.

Is this what you want?

After

I can see lots of plants, animals
And people having picnics,
I can smell lots of flowers and fresh food,
I can hear people talking
And animals rustling in the bushes.

Or this?

This is your choice!

Abigail Bernabe (11)
The Hazeley School, Milton Keynes

Carbon Footprint

I am your carbon footprint,
I follow you around,
No matter where you are,
No matter how you got there,
I am always there.

I am your carbon footprint,
I'm ever growing bigger,
I come around to haunt you,
Even when you're dying.

I am your carbon footprint,
My job is quite clear,
If you don't like me,
There's nothing you can do.

I am your carbon footprint,
I'm with you on your deathbed,
I'm with you in your house,
I'm with you in your head.

I am your carbon footprint,
I'm with you every day,
It doesn't matter if you're dead,
I will never end!

Adam Marshall (11)
The Hazeley School, Milton Keynes

Housekeeping - Haiku

Oceans blue, skies too
Ozone layer breaking through
Keep me safe and clean.

Catherine March (11)
The Hazeley School, Milton Keynes

Keep The Planet Clean

Keep the planet clean,
So it can be a glistening place for everyone!
Keep the planet clean
Then we could see the shimmering turquoise seas
And all the beautiful green land.
If we clean the planet, the seas and land will blind our eyes,
So keep the planet clean
And we won't see litter on the floor all the time.
Keep the planet clean
And live in peace.

Tom Woodroofe (11)
The Hazeley School, Milton Keynes

The Lost Soul That Nobody Knows

I could hear the rain and wind outside,
I could tell what the weather was going to be like,
So I put on my warm clothes and smile,
I go downstairs for a while.
I ate my breakfast that filled me to the top
And off out I go to my Saturday job.
As I walk along the street I see this girl who is so weak.
She isn't smiling sweet,
Instead she looks with a frown that is so bleak.
Because this girl is homeless, she has no job to go to,
No place to call home.
She didn't put on fresh new clothes,
No she didn't even get the chance to use the comb.
Where does this girl go when it's cold?
Who does she turn to when there is no one to hold?
She doesn't know when she's due her next meal,
She doesn't care or even feel.
No, this girl has given up,
She is a lost soul with no luck.
And there is me, all clean and proud
And there is her in a lonely crowd.

Shai Barrett (11)
The Hazeley School, Milton Keynes

Pollution

P ollution is ruining the world
O f course humans are doing it
L itter everywhere
L iving things are dying from pollution
U gly pollution everywhere
T ipping things away pollutes the oceans
I t is turning the world into a dump
O ceans full of rubbish
N eglect all over the world.

Courtney Doyle (12)
The Hazeley School, Milton Keynes

Litter Is Bad - Haiku

Litter is rubbish,
It's destroying our planet,
So we need to change.

Jack Hurley (11)
The Hazeley School, Milton Keynes

The World

Pollution is destroying our world.
October is getting warmer.
Levels of the sea are rising.
Ultimately countries will be lost.
Time will only tell.
Icebergs are slowly melting.
Oh how will we stop it?
Never ignore the warning - pollution is ruining the world.

Rosie Scott (12)
The Hazeley School, Milton Keynes

Recycle

R eally come on
E veryone
C ould you please do
Y our country proud
C ans, bottles, plastic stuff
L et's do a favour
E veryone start recycling!

Lewis Hope (11)
The Hazeley School, Milton Keynes

Recycling

Saving the planet,
Means being green,
Walk to your meeting,
Then turn off the heating,
So you can be good like me.

Recycling can help
Save the world too,
Encourage other people,
So it's not just you.

If you walk or cycle
To school every day,
There will be no pollution
To make the skies grey.

Being green is a really cool thing
And all you need to do
Is turn off the lighting.
If you're really good at being green,
Then you would be recycling.

Justine Connolly (11)
The Hazeley School, Milton Keynes

Let's Come Together

The forests are dying,
Pollution levels are flying,
The Earth is suffering,
Don't sit back and do nothing.
We don't want to lose the Earth forever,
So let's help and come together,
Racism has no place
Because we are all part of the human race,
We need our animals to survive,
So let's find ways to keep them alive,
So let's come together
To make the world better.

Oliver McCafferty (11)
The Hazeley School, Milton Keynes

No More Pollution

P is for petrol that fuels our cars,
O is for oil that kills all our seabirds,
L is for landfill where our rubbish is sent,
L is for life which is dying because of pollution,
U is for USA where there are big polluting cars,
T is for traffic; there is more and more,
I is for industry which generates waste,
O is for ozone; there is less and less,
N is for no. No more pollution.

Tom Flaherty (11)
The Hazeley School, Milton Keynes

Pollution

Ponds are getting polluted
Our parks have too much rubbish
Lakes are becoming marshes
Under the road there's graffiti
Timber! Too many trees are being cut down
I can help the planet
Our job to do our bit towards a healthy planet
No more poverty in Africa or anywhere.

Matthew Nelmes (11)
The Hazeley School, Milton Keynes

What Do You See?

Look out of the window,
What do you see?
A precious purple flower blooming sweetly,
Or a tall, firm apple tree?

Now look into the future,
What do you see?
Teenagers talking about knife crime while doing graffiti,
Or a shiny car spluttering by with fumes drifting up into the sky?

Now close your eyes,
Wonder, why?
Look to the sky,
How close is the sun?

How long have we got
Until it gets too hot?
What can you do to help?

Turn off the lights
And stop the fights,
Take care of the world to outstanding heights,
Help before it's too late and stop all the hate.

Megan Newman (12)
The Hazeley School, Milton Keynes

Help Me Change The World - Haikus

Crime is around us,
Stealing from shops and houses,
This is illegal!

Please use less paper,
Animals are losing homes,
Recycle paper!

Spray can graffiti,
Is under the underpaths,
This is not cool art!

Recycle your cans,
Put your litter in the bin,
Try to walk to school!

The polluting cars,
Ozone layer is thinning,
Help me change the world!

Shannon Leigh Wedley (12)
The Hazeley School, Milton Keynes

I Am The Sick Earth

My lungs are the polluted air
My brain is the cutting of the wild trees
The overflowing, polluted streams
Are my poor blood vessels
Killing the whales in the ocean,
That is the chambers of my heart.

Sian Orange (12)
The Hazeley School, Milton Keynes

The Homeless Man In Olney

The homeless man in Olney
Has a warm and kind face
You can find him in the sunshine
Sat in the same place.

The homeless man in Olney
Worked hard when he went to school
He used to help homeless charities
But now he can't use those tools.

The homeless man in Olney
Sleeps inside his one-man tent
The rain falls hard through the night
And now the tent is bent.

My mum went to Matalan
And bought me a new quilt
We gave the homeless man in Olney
New bedding to keep him warm and dry
And he said a thousand thank yous.

Lewis Orpwood (11)
The Hazeley School, Milton Keynes

Homeless

H ard as it seems, people have dreams,
O f living like kings and queens.
M any fall, fail and follow the trail,
E ach living off cold baked beans.
L ife's full of pity in cardboard city,
E veryone fends for themselves.
S ad and lonely, it's just them only,
S eems they've been left on the shelves.

Joe Lawson (11)
The Hazeley School, Milton Keynes

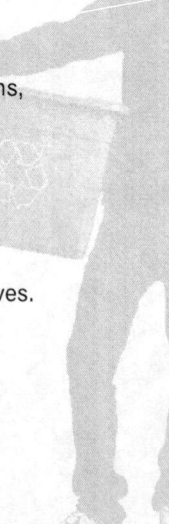

Waiting

Attentively, I sit and wait.
The curdling scream stops my little heart.
My mother told me to stay here.
Where is she?

I get used every day,
Our breed is at the brink of extinction.
When you're grown up,
Your children won't ever get to hear our shocking roars
Or see our famous natural stripes . . .
Not if you consistently take our lives away.
With pride, I am the mother of four,
I was so happy -
I was going to watch them grow from young to old,
Playing on the ice.
But now, they're locked up in a cage,
Waiting to be the fabric on your coat.
We sit and wait every day, every minute, every second,
For you to treat animals the way you want to be treated.

Rinnah Bassey (11)
The Hazeley School, Milton Keynes

Out With Racism

O bscene
U gly
T errible

W hether it's a 'joke' or not
I t's bullying
T he racists know.
H uman rights are equal to everyone, full stop.

R acism is wrong
A s everyone is human,
C ultural and has a chance to be fair.
I gnorance to personality is chosen,
S elected by prejudiced people
M ake a stand, stamp it out.

James Knight (11)
The Hazeley School, Milton Keynes

Foul!

Out in the cold someone's house is sold
Wishing they could buy but never gonna try.
No food or drink, not even a washing sink.
Getting pestered, maybe arrested. 'Move along now.'
Everywhere around, especially in the town.
What are we gonna do? Accept it, let 'em through.
Their clothes are rotten, bad; that's why they're so sad.
What about the children's health, aren't you gonna help?
We can stop it now cos it's foul!
Who's gonna help 'em? We are!

Georgia Sue Matthews (11)
Thomas Knyvett College, Ashford

The Lone Soldier

Now we pray before we become prey.
Just look at old Harry,
Now a pistol he must carry,
Alone he strides through empty battlefields,
Looking for a victory that will never come . . .

We stand here now,
Looking at the dead,
Not wishing to join them . . .

They are coming, we cannot get out,
It won't be long now
Before our lights go out . . .

James Sutherland (11)
Thomas Knyvett College, Ashford

Save The Solar System

Our planet is important to me and you,
We use it every day in what we say and do.

But it is slowly dying every day,
Because of people throwing litter instead of throwing it away.

We can help it by keeping it clean,
By picking up litter and by working as a team.

So all you have to do is pick up a can or two,
And you can help the planet for me and you.

Jade Ayers (11)
Thomas Knyvett College, Ashford

White Tiger Endangered

White tigers everywhere
All I see is snowy hair
They walk around
Without a sound
And creep out like a bear.
But today there are no sounds or sight
Which makes me want to cry.
I wait for someone to come
Nothing will come,
That makes me dumb.
I lost my family, friends and home
So please come to save me,
I am waiting for you to come.

Kista Gurung (11)
Thomas Knyvett College, Ashford

Boom!

People crying in the streets,
The siren is starting.
People run!
A house gets blown to pieces,
The evil is creeping over us.
It is all around.
Horror! Blood! Hatred!
The children are fleeing.
Planes are screeching overhead.
People are not so lucky.
The evil is spreading more and more.

Frustration! Pain! Bones!
Guns! Bombs! Grenades!
All gone off.
A house is crushing
The remains of a family!
The world is covered
With evil and threat . . .
Boom!

Arianne Dyett (11)
Thomas Knyvett College, Ashford

Nowhere

Nowhere to run
Nowhere to hide
From the deepest feeling you feel inside.
Nowhere to go
Nowhere to sleep
Open up and take a peep.
Nowhere to discover
Nowhere to lay
Everywhere is gone today.
The trees are gone
The bushes are cut
The people are coming to close us shut.
The saws are slicing
Here comes the sand
They are all coming to take over our land.
The houses are coming
The sheds are coming
The bricks are coming
The electric's coming
They're coming . . .
Us animals need somewhere to go . . .

Hayley Sewell (11)
Thomas Knyvett College, Ashford

Save Endangered Animals

Think about all those cute polar bears
They're skinned to death so they're meat with no hairs.
Think about the giant panda, nearly extinct,
Their homes are being wiped out in a blink.
Think about the penguins in the North Pole,
By taking them to zoos you're taking their souls.
Think about the black rhinos in the tall grass,
They'll be dead before a minute has passed.
Think about the orang-utans, all on their own,
You're putting them in captivity, now they're all alone.
Think about the snow leopards in the white snow,
Their numbers are getting low.
By killing the animals, you're being cruel,
It's like being sucked into the black hole.

Raisha Hussain (11)
Thomas Knyvett College, Ashford

Bullying

'Stupid little pathetic idiot'
That's what they chant at me.
It gets louder and louder every time
Just drumming, drumming, drumming away.

So what if I'm short?
Who cares if I am?
So why does it matter?
And what's it to them?

I don't know what to do.
I don't know who to tell.
I don't know who to trust.
I don't know what to say.

They're coming for me soon. I know they are.
I can't stop them. It's far too late.
What they'll bring with them, I don't know
And where I'll meet them, I dread to think.

Sarah-Jane Stedman (12)
Tormead School, Guildford

Recycling

Why do people throw me away?
Always in the wrong bin.

I'm plastic not tin,
So put me in the right bin.

Look after the world we live in,
Or it will be a rubbish bin.

Paper and card in purple,
All naughty weeds in green.

Bottles and jars in the red box,
Kitchen foil in the blue.

For now put the rest together,
So we don't upset the weather.

Helena Coombs (12)
Tormead School, Guildford

Littering

If everyone was good
The way they should
The place wouldn't be a mess
And it would pass any test.

Putting rubbish in a bin
Shouldn't be seen as a sin
I hate the gum on the street
Making the road look like a white sheet.

Bins are on every corner
Use them, don't make me a mourner
The newly cleaned streets
Looking clean, new and neat.

Oh if everyone was good
The way I know they should
The world wouldn't be a mess
And it would pass all tests.

Sarah Barrett (12)
Tormead School, Guildford

Bullying

Stalking me like I'm their prey
I'm trying to hide like a needle in hay.
Punching me as I'm their punching bag.
I get scared as I get dragged.
'Stupid', 'Pig', 'Idiot', these are a few names they call me.
Threatening me to death you see.
Why is there such a thing,
Such a thing as bullying?

Madeline Roberts (12)
Tormead School, Guildford

Bullies

They followed me home
Right up until I went round the corner
They didn't stop there though
Their words followed me into my room.

I sat there feeling hopeless
Their words rang in my head
'If you tell, I'll get you, then your family.'
They were like a song singing in my head.

I stepped out onto the balcony but all I saw was them
The three of them looking at me in disgust
I swallowed the lump in my throat
Got the knife and jumped.

Chloë Potter (12)
Tormead School, Guildford

Happiness

A brightly lit room,
Music blaring,
Talking,
Laughing,
Happiness.

Beautiful shoes,
Gorgeous dresses,
Spending,
Shopping,
Happiness.

Latest fashions,
'Must have' clothing,
Wanting,
Finding,
Happiness.

And the little child who
Works all night,
Sitting in the mud,
Fingers bleeding,
Eyes aching,
Sewing.

A brightly lit room,
Music blaring,
Talking,
Laughing,
Happiness?

Katherine Badman (12)
Tormead School, Guildford

Bullying

There was a bully in school,
Someone I used to call a 'friend',
She followed me everywhere,
As though I was unable to defend.
I never wanted to come to school,
Not after what she did,
I felt like a complete fool,
Like a useless kid,
Then I knew what I had to do,
Even though I might regret it,
I went up to a teacher
And told her everything.
I am glad I told her,
Hope that it won't happen again.
Everything is back to normal,
The way it should have been.

Müge Ercis (12)
Tormead School, Guildford

Why?

She's like a tiger so fearsome and sly
I feel so alone I just want to cry
It was the dead of night, she was ready to pounce
And I'm her prey, I need to bounce!
She's taking me somewhere, I'm not sure where
It can't be good so I need to prepare
I'm so nervous! What will she do?
I know it's going to be bad like a monster going *boo!*
We've stopped now.
She's getting out the car.
Suddenly I feel a blow in my stomach.
She's hurting me.
Why?

Katie Duxbury (12)
Tormead School, Guildford

Don't Throw It Out!

Stop, what are you doing? Don't throw it out.

That newspaper, those envelopes don't belong in the bin.
Do you know what you are doing is a great sin?
Think about the trees swaying in the breeze.
Oh lovely oxygen. Thank you wonderful trees.

Stop, what are you doing? Don't throw it out.

That wine bottle, those baked bean tins, the jar for that tea light,
They are going to a landfill site.
Please recycle the glass and tin can be reused,
This is easy, I am not confused.

Stop, what are you doing? Don't throw it out.

Apple cores, coffee grounds, eggshells and more,
Put them in your compost bin right outside your door,
Use the compost to help your flowers grow,
This is a tip you ought to know.

Stop, what are you doing? Don't throw it out.

Hopefully this poem has helped you change your ways,
Start to recycle without any delays,
This is your turn to save our planet for the next generation,
Make this your greatest donation!

Stop, what are you doing? Don't throw it out.

Stephanie Palmer (12)
Tormead School, Guildford

Because He Was There

Walking. Wolf whistling,
Down the street.

Jeering. Joking,
With his mates.

Late. Lifeless,
Stupid really.

Drunk. Dizzy,
Out of their minds.

Noise. Footsteps,
Around the block.

Faltering laughter,
Everything stops.

Face to face,
Drunk versus sane,
Confident versus scared.
One turns to run,
One reaches into their pocket.
Four step back to watch.

A flash of silver.
A scream.
Silence.

But why?
Because he was there.

Five titter away.
One lies there.

        Still.

Katherine Thomas (12)
Tormead School, Guildford

Soldier

Once I was free as a dove,
Flying in my own way,
Then one day without warning
My happiness went away.

The soldiers had come,
They arrived with no fear,
Just watching their ways
To my eye came a tear.

No soldier was given mercy,
Every day was stained with blood,
My life was filled with death and pain,
The brave left to rot in the mud.

I learned to trust no one,
Not to hear what they said,
I could never feel pain
Harshness was to rule my head.

My life ended in captivity,
Taken by the other side,
The ransom was too great,
I was branded worthless and left to die.

Once I was free as a dove,
Flying in my own way,
Then one day without warning,
My happiness went away.

Pip Scott (12)
Tormead School, Guildford

Save The Animals

If we keep killing animals to show off
Then all of them will be gone.
'So?' you might scoff
'I'll be dead then.'

But your ancestors will
Never see a tree frog
In the rainforests of Brazil
Doing whatever tree frogs do.

Or a polar bear
In the icy cold Arctic,
Taking so much care
To look after their young.

Or a cuddly panda in China
Or a mighty bald eagle
Soaring over North Carolina,
Or a lonely racoon, harming none.

They'll never see a proud wild baboon
Shaking its bum to a rhythm,
Or a desert snake slithering on a sand dune,
Or a rhino charging at an imaginary threat.

They will never see any proud beautiful animals:
Like we have never seen a dodo,
Because of others,
Who have wiped out a whole species,

For their own selfish purposes.

Victoria Marland (12)
Tormead School, Guildford

Death Of A Tree

Living in the rainforest happily,
With the other trees who are my family.
But there's a truck, what's that doing here?
One of them came last year.
It took poor Bessy, my bestest friend,
Then I watched as it drove round the bend.
An evil man comes this way now,
I hope he doesn't strike my bough.
He takes a mighty swing with his axe,
I take this time to say goodbye to Max.
As I fall from the sky,
I barely have time to say bye-bye.
Things look different from down here,
I can see the men drinking their beer.
Chop, chop, chop! I'm being cut in half.
All I can see down here is their calves.
Oww, oww, oww! It really hurts,
Now I can see one is called Burt.
Now my life is near its end,
I hope I don't start a new trend.

Abigail Whall (12)
Tormead School, Guildford

A Counsellor

A gang against one just isn't fair,
Don't kick, don't punch or even stare,
It won't get better if you go to a fair
You have to tell on your own or in pairs.

If it goes on the bully'll find you weak
Then we'll have some problems to twist and tweak
You've got to have some courageous guts
Or the bully will cover you in some awful cuts.
You finally told, now it's better than ever
Life couldn't at all just get any better.

Alice C True (12)
Tormead School, Guildford

Bullied

Isolated, all alone,
In a corner, totally unknown.
My only friend by my side,
My happiness has died inside.

Horrible, unkind,
Those words playing in my mind.
Should I tell? Maybe not,
They might start planning another plot.

A smile, a frown,
My whole world turned upside down.
Tears dripping out of my eye,
All I want to do is cry.

A bell, a glare,
Those eyes and that stare.
I stand up and try to face the day,
Too scared, I just turn away.

Isolated, all alone,
In a corner, totally unknown.
Another day goes by,
And still I feel like a tiny fly.

Caroline Davies (12)
Tormead School, Guildford

Drowning Beth

Tears trickling down her face,
Her red cheeks burnt and sore from the salty water
Flowing from her flooding eyes, drowning in tears.
Falling deeper and deeper,
Feeling the need to give up,
Sharp scars across her forehead,
Bruised from thrashings and her skin inflamed.

Hiding beneath the leaves,
In need of care,
Looking towards her bedroom window,
Frightened, tense.

It was only last night,
A scream came from downstairs,
She was alone in her bedroom
Under the duvet, terrified, petrified,
But she couldn't stay still,
Her heart was beating like a drum
Her chest was tight, she wanted to yell
To let out all her emotions and anger.

It was when she heard her dad lash out at her sister,
Who was agonising on the floor as she ran from the house,
Up to the treetops,
Where she could let it all out, and no one would find her,
She was deeply broken-hearted, a lost soul
Drowning in tears . . .

Georgia Scott (12)
Tormead School, Guildford

The Figure In The Shadows

Snow falls to the ground
A figure stands in the shadows
With his scruffy old hound
And a fate that's worse than the gallows

He's wearing ten layers of clothes
And yet his body still quakes
When the icy wind gives a chilling moan
Another tear falls as his heart breaks

The words hurl from a car window
Hobo, loser, tramp
Their hateful voices pierce his soul
As he huddles in the damp

He knows it won't be long now
Until the sun begins to rise
Yet the night is long and nothing will show
The people's cruelty he does despise

No amount of sunshine coming up
Can erase away his pain
Of living out of a coffee cup
And having nothing and nowhere to turn

This Earth is crying
Hear its plea
Hoping to regain
That old tranquillity

Before there were homeless
Before there was pain
Please hear these words
Before it's too late.

Estelle McLellan (13)
Westergate Community School, Westergate

The Call Of The Animals

The animals are calling,
Calling out, yelling and bawling,
Birds, amphibians and also mammals,
They are all endangered animals.

Some sub-species have gone,
All they want is a bond,
If we help answer their calls,
We need to help, we have the right tools.

We are lame,
The tigers, elephants and pandas are dying,
We are to blame, they need our help,
Even plants need our help just like kelp.

People are taking them from afar,
Little animals they are,
Their mums killed for meat and fur,
The family they loved now can't purr.

So here I am just to say,
Just stop this nonsense right away,
They just wait; hurt, alone and cold,
In captivity they're not very bold.

Hannah Hill (13)
Westergate Community School, Westergate

Environmental

Earth, the environment - the things we destroy!
Nature, animals - things we kill!
Vast amounts of deforestation!
I think we are turning a blind eye
Rivers filled with so much pollution!
Ozone, it wastes away like fossil fuels
Mother Nature cleans it up!
Economical - governed by power
Now we have to change to restore balance
Tomorrow is a new day!
All together we can save today
Learn to love the things we have.

Zac Rigby (13)
Westergate Community School, Westergate

So Much Craziness

Polluted water,
People are dying,
Why aren't you helping?
Open your eyes,
What type of world are we living in,
We treat our entire world,
Like a nation-wide bin.
Little boys and girls,
Under the age of five,
Living on rubbish dumps,
Trying to survive,
Do your best to help the nation,
Don't destroy God's creation.

Danni Noble (13)
Westergate Community School, Westergate

Poverty

No food, no water, nowhere to live
What can we do, what can we give?
Dying by the second . . .
Decreasing population . . .
AIDS, HIV, hunger
It's a disgrace to the nation.

Dying of hunger, dying of thirst
Kids walking and sleeping on the dumps,
Left there for weeks maybe months.
It's time we start appreciating
All the stuff we have,
All the food we're eating.

Not for them designer labels,
Christmas gifts and laden tables.
Hunger pains are all they have
To see them through the long cold night,
No blankets or soft beds for them
Just cold hard earth until morning light.

Lianne Cronk (13)
Westergate Community School, Westergate

What If . . .

What if you woke in poverty each day?
What if you could just never have your say?

What if you knew how your children would live?
How does it feel that they may not survive?
Possibly not even until they are five,
Like one in six of those in poverty.

What if you knew how hungry they would feel?
You see for yourself what would be their fate,
Just knowing they would be well underweight,
Like a third of those in poverty.

What if you saw them suffer all day long?
Suffer from diseases like malnutrition,
How could they bear such a harsh condition?
Can you imagine what it would be like?

What if you knew just how bad it would be?
What if you lived with AIDS or malaria,
Living in a rural African area,
As ninety million people there do?

What if you knew how many have died today?
When more than 30,000 children have died today,
And for that what can you possibly say,
Each 3 seconds you read this another dies!

Keziah Norrell (13)
Westergate Community School, Westergate

Pollution

P ollution
O ver the world everyone is polluting
L ots of engines stopping and starting
L itres of valuable petrol being wasted
U nderstand now we need to do something about this
T urn off your engines when you're not moving
I t's time for you to do your bit
O ver time the Earth will die
N ow we need to altogether stop *polluting*.

Cameron Howell-McIntyre (13)
Westergate Community School, Westergate

Act Now!

Poverty is manmade,
Many suffer,
Whilst others get paid.

Poverty destroys lives
Worldwide
Sons, husbands,
Daughters, wives.

This means every
3 seconds a child dies
You work out how many lives.

People accept poverty
As a 21st century thing
What kind of world are we living in?

People say I
Don't know what to do?
25p
Hasn't that given you a clue?

Poverty is here to stay
Unless you help
By doing something today.

It's time that we make amends
You can help . . .
To ensure this poverty *ends!*

This generation holds the key
To ending worldwide poverty!

Act now.

'We live in a broken world, which has never been healthier, wealthier or bizarrely free of conflict, but all over the world, people die of want. It's not only intellectually absurd but also morally repulsive'.
(Sir Bob Geldof)

Faith Poston-Miles (13)
Westergate Community School, Westergate

Recycling The True Story

Every person
In the UK
Throws their bodyweight
Of rubbish away

This happens
Every year,
Stop it now
Keep it clear

Recycling is hard
For everyone,
Do your bit
Get the job done

Separate
Good from bad,
Keep it tidy
Don't be sad

It's not a chore
No it's not,
Help the world
Clean the slop

I've done my bit
Now it's you,
Prove you know
That it's true.

Jake Simpson (13)
Westergate Community School, Westergate

The Homeless Poem

Think of how lucky we are
People travel from near and far
They haven't got a bike or a car
They walk barefoot on the tar.

Think of how much food we eat
Think of our houses warm with heat
There's a lot to be told so take a seat
Think of the homeless you see in the street.

Do you really think this is fair?
Are you so heartless that you don't care?
For me to see them sitting there
So skinny and heartbroken, that I can't bear.

Sitting in the cold with a new baby born
Wishing they could be somewhere warm
Always trying to sleep before it's dawn
Wearing tatty clothes all shabby and worn.

A man sits there with his old wet hound
Looking around but there's no food to be found
Listening to the city's sound
Trying to sleep on the cold wet ground.

He wanders around the corner shop
Clinging on to his baggy top
His hair all tangled like a mop
He frowns as his hopes finally drop.

There he lies still
He wakes to the sound of a drill
He coughs, as he is ill
People watch as his life goes downhill.

Nicola Ann Parfoot (13)
Westergate Community School, Westergate

Now Black Not White

I scan the sky
The aurora sings,
The folding curtains
Spread their wings
The reflection on the remaining ice
Tainted by cream,
That was once white.

Silent and still
A polluted life lies,
Unnaturally thin with
Black staring eyes,
The innocent are suffering
The purest of pure,
Now grey, not white.

Dirty seagulls forage meat
From the scum below,
Giant tin cans and oil spills
Infect the ice and snow,
In amongst this pillaged land
Is a sinless creature's home,
Now ebony, not white.

All around nature is screaming
The aurora is a sign,
Polar bears dying
And young seals crying,
The pollution has to stop
If not now
Then our future's decided,
It'll be black not white.

Gemma Williams (13)
Westergate Community School, Westergate

Litter Causes Pollution

Everywhere I go,
A carpet of infection covers the ground,
Everywhere I go,
There's a crunching sound
That is litter beneath my feet,
Where does it come from?
Lives at stake,
But not just ours,
Animals die from oil 'n' tar,
Litter causes pollution.

Carbon dioxide produced by cars,
Destroying the world, close and far,
Vast amounts of dark grey smoke,
Containing diseases that will make you choke,
Producing gases, this is true,
I can make a difference and so can you.

Ben Root (13)
Westergate Community School, Westergate

The Dog

I dread for when my owner gets back
I know for no reason I will get smacked
The hurt, the loss, the smacks, the pain
I know I definitely will not gain
I know I'm not in the wrong
He wins 'cause he is so strong
The life I've lost, the pain he's caused
He even stands on my paws
All I need is some friendly help
I long to have love to be smelt
The love I need, the lovely talk,
I'm just a dog who needs love and to be walked.

Holly Anne MacWhirter (13)
Westergate Community School, Westergate

Change The World

The polluting fumes kill the air,
People all around me they just don't care,
The Earth turns from green to black,
We all carry pollution on our back.

The Earth's heat starts to rise,
Life around me starts to die,
Each day I wonder what we have done,
What happened to us - what have we become?

Everywhere around litter fills this place,
This madness has to stop before we wipe out the human race,
Let's change the world and make things right,
The battle's just begun - get ready to fight.

Danny Vaughan (13)
Westergate Community School, Westergate

How About A World

How about a world of dirt?
How about a world of peace?
Or rather a world of hurt,
Or would you rather cease?

How about a world of calm?
How about a world of destruction?
Or keep nature's charm,
Or rather a world of corruption.

We all don't seem to mind,
We don't even care,
It's not very kind
It's not fair.

We all just blow it away
Earth has become a killing field,
Really there is another way,
We have the power we just need to yield.

Black clouds surround us,
And all it does is rain
So don't take a car, take a bus
We don't seem to have a brain.

Jake Enticott (14)
Westergate Community School, Westergate

Band Together Forever

Burning planes,
Blown out lanes,
Giving their thanks
To iron tanks.

Bombs are coming,
Men are gunning.
Explosions bring death,
Till there's not one breath.

Searing hot lead,
Flying past my head.
And burning iron rain,
Bringing utmost pain.

They say we go to glory,
Instead it's all gory.
We fight for a politician,
Who says it's our mission.

But tell me how,
We can make peace now.
When leaders make more enemies,
Oblivious to their people's pleas.

If we band together,
Be allies forever
Then all this killing and all this war,
Will be gone for evermore.

Then all this pain and all this sorrow,
Will be diminished for a new tomorrow.
When this war is over,
We won't need a four-leaf clover.

The nukes we launched are not forgotten,
The world we have is smoggy and rotten.
Now what we have left should be preserved,
Because our time is not reserved.

Our world can be clean,
Like a soft silver sheen.
And then we shall have for evermore
The world we've all been waiting for

Michael Long (13)
Westergate Community School, Westergate

Homeless

I lie alone
Frozen to the bone
The darkness of night
There is no light.

I watch the people walking by
Businessmen sneer and women sigh
If only they could feel my pain
They live a life of total gain.

Children run by having fun
But where I am there is no sun
Misery is all I am
It is my life, who I am.

There they are all mighty and high
On the floor here I lie
They don't give me a second glance
Not a word, not a chance.

So every time you sidle by
Think of me, it's here I lie
I bet you wonder why I hope
But I have just learnt to cope.

No longer do I feel despair
I've learnt that people just don't care.

Kathryn Follis (13)
Westergate Community School, Westergate

Endangered Animals

Come and give them a helping hand,
The animals will die without you,
We also need to help save their land.
What about the black rhinos,
We kill them for their horns, why though?
The giant pandas could be facing extinction
Because of us,
But we're not making a big fuss,
There are only 6,000 tigers remaining in the wild,
So why don't we treat them like a child?
Why are these alligator snapping turtles
Being killed for their meat?
Do you not think we already have enough to eat?
Why are we trading the hawksbill turtle shell?
Without a home it would be hell,
Why are these beautifully coloured parrots
Being kept as pets?
Extinction is what the green-cheeked parrots fret,
Why are we stripping the prized fins
Off the mako shark?
And then chucking them back in
To die in the depths,
To help stop all of this,
Make sure the animals harsh future is stopped,
Then finally the animals can live in bliss.

Gemma Thomas (13)
Westergate Community School, Westergate

No Way Back

Every puff of smoke
Every bomb set off
Every second I sit . . . I sense the world's about to cough

Thundering clouds charge from chimneys
Mountain tops reduced to quarries,
All the recycling has gone out the door,
We've never seen this much pollution before.

The world before, peaceful and tranquil
Now our waste goes straight to the landfill,
We used to live in an urban culture,
That's all eaten up by the pollution-like-vulture.

Flowering fields to barren deserts,
A world of horror, a world of hurt,
Iridescent lakes to oil pits,
We will find a way, we shall never quit.

All this pollution summed up in one,
The dread hasn't ended, it has just begun.

Bill Bailey (13)
Westergate Community School, Westergate

Why Does War Commence?

What has the world done?
Why does everything involve a gun?
When will the war end?
It's going to take a lot to mend.

Last night I was sleeping
While my life I was keeping
I was lying there weeping
Wondering when my life would end.

Why does this commence?
Is it because we have no defence?
Why is everything such an offence?
When will all this come to a grinding end!

I was in my home
Crying on the phone
Asking my friend if she had known
Why this war has been going on?

They're fighting for us and risking their lives
They could get stabbed by a knife.
War
What is it good for?
War...
When will it stop?

Emma Morphy (13)
Westergate Community School, Westergate

What Can We Do?

People are in trouble
And the world is too,
But we're just small
What could we do?

Well doing small things
Can go very far,
Like riding your bike
And not using the car,
Or just giving money

To help out the poor,
Or even paying tribute
To those at war,
So with all of us joined together,
We can make tomorrow not perfect but better!

Daniel Morgan (13)
Westergate Community School, Westergate

Racism

R acist people can be put in jail
A ll racist people should be
C rime, yes it's very bad.
I t leaves people upset and sad
S uicide it can cause.
M any people hurt and distraught.

Ruby Nicholls (11)
Wheatley Park School, Oxford

Change

Animals in small cramped cages,
See what you are doing?
Just stop all the different stages,
Animal cruelty does need changing.

Rubbish flying out of car windows,
Litter on the streets
Why are people doing this?
The world is incomplete.

Recycling is not hard,
An easy thing to do.
But they don't care - it's not them,
That act the way they do . . .
So please just stop!

Issy Standley (11)
Wheatley Park School, Oxford

The World

T rees are being cut down
H omeless people living on streets
E lectricity used when not needed
　　　　　　we can turn this around.

W orking footballers never come cheap
O il burning in people's cars
R ecycle - it's better for our world
L iving people in poverty
D on't kill animals for fur, it's cruel.

Ana Majdi (11)
Wheatley Park School, Oxford

Recycle

R ecycling, you should do it for life
E nough people are living by the knife
C an you see what we've done?
Y ou are all living by the gun
C an we change?
L isten to me
E veryone should recycle for you and for me.

Shakur Gabbidon-Williams (11)
Wheatley Park School, Oxford

What's Going On!

What's going on? Litter, pollution, war,
Endangered animals and more,
These bad things should not be happening,
The world brings good and we bring bad,
This is making most of us sad,
In return help the world out and
Recycle, recycle, recycle!

Regan Cullen (11)
Wheatley Park School, Oxford

Change

C ars on the roads for no reason.
H ate, greed, cruelty and treason
A nimals are dying every day
N o one's doing stuff about it, that's what I've got to say
G o and be brave, go and show your face
E veryone can try and make the world a better place.

Davy Byrne (11)
Wheatley Park School, Oxford

What Makes Me Angry?

What makes me angry?
You're wasting water,
You're killing trees,
You're experimenting on animals,
That's what makes me angry!

What makes me angry?
You're covering Earth with litter,
You're driving not walking,
You're having war with no reason,
That's what makes me angry!

So do something to change this!

Jessie Green (11)
Wheatley Park School, Oxford

Why Do We Suffer In Silence?

Money in the world
Adventures in life
People being successful
New life on Earth.

Politicians not caring
Not thinking of anyone else
Taking things for granted
All 'do as I say not do as I do'.

Poor suffering people
Nobody who cares
Suffering in silence
People taking money and happiness for granted.

Why can't anyone see
What's happening today?
Why can't anyone see
That we're all dying slowly.

Victoria Montgomery (11)
Wheatley Park School, Oxford

Young Writers Information

We hope you have enjoyed reading this book - and that you will continue to enjoy it in the coming years.
If you like reading and writing poetry drop us a line, or give us a call, and we'll send you a free information pack.
Alternatively if you would like to order further copies of this book or any of our other titles, then please give us a call or log onto our website at www.youngwriters.co.uk

Young Writers Information
Remus House
Coltsfoot Drive
Peterborough
PE2 9JX
(01733) 890066